Let HIM
Chase
YOU

A Simple Guide For Women Who Want Both Long-Lasting Love and Respect in Their Relationships with Men

by
L. LYNN GILLIARD

Let *Him* Chase *You*
Published by: Venup Publishing

LetHimChaseYou.com

Copyright 2013 L. Lynn Gilliard
All rights reserved.
ISBN 978-0-9836392-2-0

Disclaimer: This guide is written for informational and educational purposes only. No warranty or guarantee is offered to the reader as to the effects of using the contents of this book. Each situation is different and thus, results vary. The author and publisher do not assume and hereby disclaim any liability to any party.

Neither the author, publisher or any associated entities assume any responsibility for errors, omissions, or contrary interpretations of the subject matter herein. The views expressed herein are those of the author alone and shouldn't be taken as expert instruction or a command. Each reader is

fully responsible for his or her own actions.

TABLE OF CONTENTS

EVE'S STORY

15 days have gone by since their first date. 3 days have gone by since he last called or texted her. 7 days have gone by since he last set up a date with her.

And it just so happens that 7 days have gone by since they first had sex.

Finally, on the 8th day of sitting by quietly waiting for a date invitation, Eve decides to break down and call him.

"I just don't think I'm ready for anything serious right now. I'm not ready to date (insert other excuse)," Thomas says when she asks him what's going on. "We can still hang out sometimes though."

Eve and Thomas have sex a couple more times -- that's what he really meant by "hanging out" after all. Then he completely "ghosts" her. No replies, no contact.

5 weeks later Eve finds out through Facebook that Thomas is "in a relationship" with another girl he just met.

Why did Thomas make the other girl his girlfriend after a short period of time but only thought Eve was fit to be his "friend with benefits?"

Keep reading this guide to find out exactly why, and how you can avoid being treated like Eve in the future.

A Man's Hierarchy of Desires/Needs in a Woman

A Looker
A Lover
A Supporter Who Believes in Him
A Friend and Confidant

A Woman's Hierarchy of Desires/Needs in a Man

A Protector
A Provider
A Looker/Lover
A Friend and Confidant

Why I'm Writing This Guide

A lot of relationship experts teach women how to "catch" a man, as if he is the prize and you as the woman should be the pursuer. Therein lies a lot of the dysfunction and confusion that many women and men have when it comes to dating and relationships today. The roles are all screwed up. Men are by nature supposed to be the chasers in heterosexual relationships.

To be clear, I am not a relationship expert; I am just a very attentive observer who studies human relationships and interactions daily. I have unfortunately seen plenty of relationships go sour. I've seen a lot of my woman friends get played, "pumped and dumped" (used for sex and then dumped or ignored) and used up by men in other ways. And of course, I have experienced the same things.

It's pretty obvious why these things happen but sometimes we women don't want to own up to our own roles in the situations—we just place blame on the guy for being a jerk. And yeah, he is a jerk for taking advantage of you with no intention of going much further with you. But if the same thing happens again, and again, and again, with different guys, some self-reflection is in order.

This was my story for a long time. I threw pity parties whenever a man suddenly and unexpectedly exited from my life. I was angry at the guy for "letting me down," but I didn't want to own up to my OWN role in what transpired. Stay tuned for a few juicy stories from my past, and yes I will be spilling a little bit of tea.

It's all about choices. The choices we make as women. Choices in how we proceed or *if* we proceed with a relationship, choices in how we act and react while dating and also the TYPE of men we choose to deal with in the first place.

While I'm not currently married (and now taking my sweet sweet time before going down that road again), I was engaged to be married to an awesome man at one point who unfortunately passed away. We had some major challenges in our relationship in the beginning, but we overcame them and eventually bonded. He was deeply in love with me (and I him), so I do know what it takes to get a man to fall for you to the point where he wants you to walk down the aisle toward him.

After a number of dating failures, I finally discovered a number of revelations that have completely changed my perspective about men and dating. I am now successfully dating again, all on my own terms and confident that my next life partner / soul mate is going to walk into my life exactly at the right time. That's a big change from being curled up in my bed depressed, and having pity parties because I thought no one cared about me.

As soon as I began implementing the ideas that I lay out in this book into my dating life, I noticed that men began to flock around me. I became the chooser, instead of feeling as if I needed to work harder to get chosen.

I'm writing this guide now because I'm very concerned about the relations between heterosexual men and women. The new trend is to find a "friend with benefits" and pretend that your feelings and emotions don't really matter on a day-to-day basis. I call BS on the idea of "friends with benefits" and I'll tell you why in a little bit.

It seems that there is more and more of a bitter divide between men and women, but I believe it is fixable. The marriage rate is declining across the board, which some think is just a sign of progression or evolution, but I think it is actually just a sign of more people being disconnected from each other. Negative past experiences and anger are holding us back from finding honest, secure, unconditional, peaceful love with each other.

The keys to overcoming this bitter divide are as follows:

1) Understand what YOU may be doing wrong in your relationships and the dating process
2) Learn to love yourself, truly and fully
3) Accept responsibility for your poor life choices instead of continuing to point the finger at others and finally
4) Make better choices in mates and in the way you deal with them in the future.

This advice goes for both sexes, but this guide specifically addresses women and dating.

Self-Esteem and Dating

I expand on this more later on in this guide, but I believe that a lot of the crap that women put up with in relationships and friends with benefits situations is simply due to a lack of self-esteem and self-love.

We don't think that we're enough. We don't think that we deserve a real relationship. We don't think that anyone could ever really love us.

But once you overcome these negative thoughts, the world opens up to you—not just in dating but everything in life. When you truly believe in yourself and the power of your womanhood, everyone else starts to believe it too. **Self-love** is the very first step to a real love-filled relationship with another person.

You're Single Because You Do "Stupid" Things
(Don't be offended, I'm not saying you're a dumb person. My definition of stupid is simply this: having an idea of what is the right way to do something but still choosing to do the opposite. Usually it is due to ignorance, arrogance, brainwashing, insecurity or fear.)

There is an imbalance when it comes to relationships between men and women. Bottom line, a lot of women have given men all of their power. The media is partly to blame for pressuring women to get married and making them feel less womanly if they don't have a man and 2.5 kids. On the other hand, men prioritize other goals, like pursuing a successful career and adventuring through life.

Men also have a lot of power over women because too many women are simply too emotional, too soon when it comes to love and relationships. We give too much (sometimes everything) but don't demand much in return. Many women are desperate for the attention of men, but most men are not as *openly* desirable of the attention of women. The result is a generation of men who don't feel that they have to do much to get and keep a woman.

I've observed that the power imbalance is starting to shift a bit as more women are starting to make more money, prioritize their careers and focus on bettering themselves. But there are still a lot of women out there who seem to be very confused about men.

The main issue is that women must set stricter boundaries when dealing with men. We can have a relationship while maintaining our dignity and self-respect in the process.

I love men. But I also know that some of them will take what they're offered without feeling any obligation to give anything in return. So if you're offering up sex, attention, home cooked meals, wifely deeds and your whole heart without first demanding what *you* want, you can't be surprised when a guy takes it all and runs.

You're reading this book because you're tired of being a friend with benefits. You're tired of being "pumped and dumped." You don't want to wake up one day at age 70 hoping that your occasional booty call at the senior home will text you. You want love and the undivided attention of one man who desires you so strongly that he wants to marry you one day. At the very least, you want a serious boyfriend.

Well, to achieve this, you're going to have to get serious about changing your bad habits when it comes to men. Take the time to marinate on the words in this guide. If you have the audio version, listen to it on your phone, while working, while in your car, while cooking or while working out as many times as it takes to absorb the information.

While the ideas presented in this guide may not apply to every woman, every man or every situation, they ring true for most people who are dating. The VERY first step to changing your relationships is changing your mindset.

Change your mind, change your life!

Key Takeaways:

- 💜 If you have the same results with different guys, time and again, some self-reflection is in order
- 💜 There is a bitter divide between men and women that can be resolved with understanding and taking responsibility for our roles in the mess (both men AND women)
- 💜 Lack of self-esteem is the reason why many women settle for unfulfilling relationships
- 💜 If you think that giving up all of yourself will compel a man do anything more than take from you, you're wrong

Chapter 1:

Why I Say "Friends with Benefits" SUCKS... At Least for Women

*F*riends with benefits (FWB) is a "relationship status" (I feel it is even a stretch to call it that) that I believe is destroying the possibility for healthy connections between young people all over the country. It basically takes all emotion and feeling out of a relationship and only focuses on physical contact. In fact, the only "benefit" of a friends with benefits relationship is sex.

A friends with benefits relationship usually benefits the guy and ultimately puts a burden on the woman.

For one, most people who enter into these relationships are not really friends. In most cases they barely even know each other. There is no real friendship to begin with. In some cases they don't even know each other's last names.

Secondly, being that women tend to associate sex

1

with emotions and men do not, women are almost always hurt when they become friends with benefits. The more sex they have, the more attached they get to the "relationship." On the other hand, the guy is just as disassociated with his emotions as he was the first time they had sex.

Remember the hierarchy of needs for women that I wrote at the beginning of this guide:

A Woman's Hierarchy of Desires/Needs in a Man
A Protector
A Provider
A Looker/Lover
A Friend and Confidant

The need for a lover is usually low on that list of priorities (of course the order varies for different types of women, but this is generally the case). I put friends at the end of the list, because women already have girlfriends to confide in. They want a man for other things.

So the bottom line here is that in a friends with benefits relationship, the woman is getting little to nothing of what she really desires and needs from a man.

Why Women Get Silly and Insecure After Sex

You may wonder why women tend to get more and more insecure in the days after a first sexual experience. We start questioning if he really likes us. Will he call? Was the sex good enough for him? Does he now think of you as a slut?

Well it turns out that a biological reaction is involved in this. When a woman has sex with a man her body releases a chemical called oxytocin. This chemical causes a woman to develop an emotional attachment to the guy she has just been intimate with. Men release this chemical after sex also, but their high levels of testosterone help balance it out, while the estrogen in women increases the effects of this chemical. The purpose of the chemical is to help the two people bond, but unfortunately it seems to be much more effective on women.

This is why FWB or sex on the first date is not a smart idea for most women but it's great for the guy, who doesn't experience the same feelings of attachment.

Once You Accept FWB, Hey, It Is What It Is

If I was asked to bet on a FWB relationship turning into a serious relationship, I'd definitely pass. The chance that this type of arrangement will become something real is not very promising because it has a bad foundation. If you decide to be someone's FWB, you had better go into it with a clear mindset and understanding that "it is what it is" and that's probably all it will ever be until you meet someone new (or he does).

If you are tired of being delegated as a FWB and never a girlfriend, keep reading this guide to understand why it keeps happening and what you can do to stop the cycle.

Insanity is doing the same thing over and over while expecting a different result.

Are You Really Ready for Love from Another Person?

A lot of women are looking for someone to love them and complete them.

The problem is, they don't even fully love themselves. How can you expect someone else to love you the way you ought to be loved if you haven't even learned how to love your own self?

Men can sense when you don't have self worth, self-love or self-confidence. The decent ones will leave you alone while the bad guys will take advantage of you first, then leave you alone, in an even worse state than before.

Email **loveletter@lethimchaseyou.com**
to receive a free copy of my very special
LOVE LETTER. Print it (it's a PDF), fill it
out and post it on your mirror.

*"You yourself, as much as anybody in the
entire universe, deserve your love and
affection."*
- Buddha

This guide is not about tricking men or using a strict
play-by-play routine to get exactly what you want
from men. That stuff doesn't work in the long run.

It's about simply knowing your worth as a woman
and prioritizing your needs as a woman. Only when
you do this can you begin and maintain a fruitful
relationship with a decent man. Only when you honestly believe that you are a prize will men start to
believe that you are a prize too.

Women who do not believe in their worth settle for
friends with benefits arrangements, booty calls and
no titles. They fool themselves into thinking that this
is enough. But when he leaves the bed and you're left
alone with your thoughts, the truth comes out.

Women need more than just sex.

We also need security and emotional support.

When you have insight into how men think and operate as well as control over your emotions, you'll relax and look at love and relationships with a much clearer mind. You might even discover that a serious relationship isn't exactly what you want at this very moment in your life.

But if you do, meeting a great man to settle down with and start a real, healthy relationship is a four-step process:

1) Deciding that that's really what you want at this time in your life
2) Changing your thoughts, words and behaviors so that you can attract more great men into your life if you do want a relationship
3) Listening to your intuition and saying "no thanks" to the guys who you know aren't right for you as soon as possible (I call these guys "rocks")
4) Bonding with one of the great men that you meet along the way (I call these men "gems"), and committing to him (and him to you of course)

If any of these steps are missing, it's difficult if not impossible to have a healthy long-term relationship with a man.

In the next section I give you a run down of some of my own past relationship blunders, and later on I'll explain how missing one or more of these steps kept me stuck in the same bad cycle for years.

Key Takeaways:

- 💜 People in friends with benefits relationships aren't really friends
- 💜 A chemical called oxytocin reacts with estrogen, making women more attached than men after sex
- 💜 Love who you are - fill out the LOVE LETTER to yourself and keep it handy
- 💜 Women need more than sex to be happy
- 💜 There are four general steps to meeting a great man and settling down—deciding what you want, changing your mind toward positive thoughts, listening to your intuition and forming a bond with the RIGHT type of guy

CHAPTER 2

My Story

So that you'll understand that I can personally relate to your pain as a chronically single woman on the dating scene, I present to you three situations that I've personally experienced with three different men who eventually dumped or "ghosted" me (ghosting is when someone suddenly stops calling for no apparent reason).

After telling you these stories I will explain in more detail exactly what I did wrong to cause each breakup.

The Young Sex-Obsessed Guy

For a time I dated a 22-year-old guy (I was over five years older than him at the time). He was really infatuated with me at first. He worked a low paying blue-collar job. He lived with his parents, which isn't that unusual for a guy in his early twenties. I didn't complain.

The first two months that we dated he became so enthralled with me that he actually talked about the idea of getting married. He said my first name with his last name to see how it would sound. He took me out to dinner several times. He would text me early in the morning, like 7am early, just to tell me to have a beautiful day. He called me his princess. We were happy and getting along nicely. I saw him twice a week and talked to him on the phone just about every day.

Then one day he suggested that we finally take it to the next level and become intimate. Since he lived with his parents and my living situation was also complicated at the time, he suggested that we get a hotel room. I agreed to meet him.

We continued to talk and date after that, and then one day I suggested that I pay for the hotel for us to hang out together. I was worried that he was spending all of his money (which wasn't very long) on our dating and wanted to make a gesture to show him that I was a "good woman."

We got together again, but for some reason everything changed after that. I didn't hear from him for about a week. When I finally heard from him, he made up a silly excuse for why he couldn't call me. I didn't believe him and in the heat of the moment I broke up with him. I thought he would try to win me back... but he didn't. Instead, he just began texting me once in a while, late at night, asking me to come meet him. Sometimes I would agree, other times I would ignore his calls. After months of this nonsense I finally realized I was being played as a booty call slash friend with benefits and gave up on the whole thing. He didn't seem bothered at all.

The Baby Daddy

I met a guy online who was my same age. He was okay-looking, tall, laid back, sweet and chivalrous, which I like in a guy, so I was interested. He was very impressed with how I looked in person. He was a perfect gentleman, refusing to let me pay on our dates. He was a creative person, which was also a major turn on for me. I thought I might have found a winner.

But I always caught him staring at my cleavage on our dates and it was obvious that there was some serious sexual tension between us from the beginning.

He waited until our second date to tell me that he had a mini-team of young children, one that was only born a couple of years before, all by the same mother. He also told me that he had had an off and on relationship with his baby's mother for over a decade. He asked if that was okay, that I could run if I wanted to. I said, "no problem, I love kids."

Later on he also admitted to me that he lived with his parents. He was in a transitional period after breaking up with his baby's mother yet again. But he had a good job and was a gentleman, so I didn't look down on him for this.

Despite all these red flags, I decided to continue dating him. The very next contact I received from him was to request if we could get a hotel room. At first I said no, that it was too soon for that, but then for some reason I changed my mind and agreed to meet him. After being intimate, I felt that we might have a connection. We went out on another date and I told him that I felt comfortable enough to invite him over to my place.

The next day, I decided to go online and check out his Facebook profile. His main picture was one of him and who I presume to be his baby's mother together. I thought that was really strange, being that he was now dating me and claimed to be completely over her, but I didn't confront him about it.

A couple of days after that, I texted him to let him know he could come over again that next day. He agreed and said he really needed to see me. That next day he texted and said he was held over with his kids and that their mother was playing games with him. We postponed until the next day.

The next day he called me and told me about all of his baby momma drama. Instead of hanging out with me the night before, he had been over his baby momma's house arguing until the wee hours of the morning. I sat there thinking, "this guy still wants his baby's mother. I don't know why I didn't see it before." A couple of hours later my thoughts were confirmed— he called me again, saying that he wasn't ready to date anyone because he had to deal with his kids. I translated this as: "I need to get my baby momma back." And that was the end of that.

Noticing a pattern here yet?

The Narcissistic City Guy

This was another young guy. He told me he was 26 when he was actually 20 (almost a decade younger than me at the time). Despite his age, he was actually pretty mature for his age. He had a very good job as a programmer and I was impressed with him. The downside of that was that he was a little pig-headed and narcissistic.

After just a few weeks of dating he made it official with me—he wanted to be my boyfriend. We talked every day, then one day he made a very controversial comment that I didn't like and we got into a big argument. We broke up and stopped talking.

A few months later he contacted me out of the blue and we started dating again, but this time it was much different. Now everything was mostly about sex. I would come to his apartment, have sex and leave in the morning. Occasionally he would take me to dinner.

We had another major point of disagreement—using protection during sex. To summarize, I wanted to use protection and he did not. It seemed as if we were having a lot of disagreements about basic things. It was almost as if he was trying to set me off. Then after spending a beautiful night together one evening, he "ghosted" me (disappeared and stop calling and texting out of the blue).

I finally called him to find out what was going on and he told me that we wouldn't work together. I literally cursed him out and then never spoke to him again.

Keep reading this guide for a complete analysis of what I did wrong in each of these cases. But first, let's talk a little about men, women and relationships in general.

CHAPTER 3

He's "In Love" With a Stripperrrr

A lot of women wonder why seemingly good men go for trashy, crazy, messy women, strippers and bad girls, only to be dumped, used and left bitter in the end.

Yes, it's sometimes because they're shallow and confused. But more specifically it's because of their hierarchy of values when it comes to women. Again, here it is:

A Man's Hierarchy of Desires/Needs in a Woman

A Looker

A Lover

A Supporter Who Believes in Him

A Friend and Confidant

15

Most men care very little about whether you are a good catch (a potential confidant, friend and supportive woman) or not early on in getting to know you. They don't care if you're a good girl at all at that point.

First and foremost they care if you meet or exceed their particular ideal of beauty and are sexually attractive. If you meet or exceed the first two points on that list above, chances are that he's gonna stick around for a little while. So that's why a trampy but beautiful stripper who uses and abuses men will have a serious boyfriend while an average-looking, plain Jane, reserved woman who cooks, works and respects men might be tossed aside like she is the trash.

His Story

Let's talk about what happens when a so-called decent guy falls under the spell of a bad girl. She is sexy, beautiful and keeps him on his toes. He knows that she doesn't really want him for who he is, but the allure of the challenge keeps him interested.

Soon enough, this seemingly decent guy gets burned by the stripper, whether it be for money or getting dumped for a bad boy. Sometimes the guy even has an out of wedlock baby by this woman, who probably has little concern for using protection or being sexually responsible. He might even contract something from the woman. In a worst-case scenario (by many accounts) he'll marry one of these women and really get taken to the cleaners. After this happens, the seemingly decent guy becomes angry guy. He's anti-relationship, anti-marriage and anti-women. He has a hard time admitting that it was his **bad choice in a woman** that caused the drama.

He becomes bitter. Then he takes it all out on every woman after that, including the good ones.

This is why there are a lot of angry and bitter men out there who complain about gold diggers and women who want "bad boys." There is a good chance that this exact sequence of events happened to them at some point in their lives. They fell in love (usually just lust) with a stripper or a bad girl and got burned bad. They ignored the need for a supporter-believer-friend and opted for the looker-lover.

After being burned, these men come to believe that playing women is the answer. But playing women and giving up on love means that they will probably be alone and bitter OR have to settle for the same type of gold digging woman in order to have the company of a desirable woman later on in life. Take a look at the majority of men over 40 or 50 and how they seem to scramble for a decent non-gold digging grown woman, but all they keep getting are gold-diggers, users or desperate young girls. (By the way, these men are what I call "rocks" and should be tossed away before they have the chance to turn your life in a similar direction. Misery loves company—see chapter 8)

Beauty and Sex Appeal Hold a Lot of Weight for Men

This general dynamic has been going on since childhood, hasn't it? Boys pick on the mild-mannered good girls in school but go crazy over the pretty mean girls.

The hierarchy of desires is also why some men will pursue a really beautiful woman for years even though she's obviously not interested in sex with him. He would probably settle for a sexless relationship just so he can have a looker on his arm. Eye candy and the mere hope of getting sex one day is enough to keep some men interested because looks are at the top of their list of desires in a woman.

This is why I feel comfortable stating that looks are firmly at the top of the priority list for men when it comes to women.

Unfortunately, the average man doesn't really care that you are a good woman when you first meet. He doesn't care that you are the type of woman who will take care of him in old age instead of using him for his money and then leaving. Most men can't see that far into the future. Right now many younger men, ages 20-45, just want a beautiful sexy woman who is going to make them feel good about themselves superficially.

Your task is weed out the bad ones who can't see the forest for the trees, focus on the good guys with great potential, and value and respect yourself in the process.

Key Takeaways:

- ❤ A lot of men go for strippers and bad girls because they give them the top two desires on their list of priorities—looks and good sex.

- ❤ The fact that you're a "good girl" doesn't matter to these men (at least not as far as first impressions) because they want the excitement of being with a bad girl—even when it hurts them.

CHAPTER 4

Understanding More About Men

*B*efore we go forward, it's important that you gain a little more of an understanding of men. Unlike women, in most cases a man will only take action on something that benefits him in some way. Men are more logical than emotional. That goes for just about everything, from work to romantic relationships.

A man will rarely do something "just because." It's part of the reason why men are still dominant in many areas of life—they know what they want, they know why they want it and they boldly go forward with their plan to claim it. They also don't feel bad about it, not one bit.

A woman will do favors for a man who she doesn't even really know "just because" or out of desperation hoping that it will make him love her.

Some men do favors for women expecting sex at some point. Or if you're sexy and beautiful they want to take you around town like a trophy to show off to friends and other men. Or the user guys will ask you for a loan at some point or want to move into your place. OR the guy's family is pressuring him to FINALLY get married to a nice girl, so he's going to go right out there and marry the first woman he finds. Or he'll buy you an expensive dress and shoes so that you can wear it to his work affair and help him get that promotion.

The point is that men don't usually do things just because they are motivated by their feelings, common sense or chivalry. They do things because they have a goal that they want to achieve, whether it is sex, acceptance, accomplishment or having someone to take care of them.

The only exception to this rule is when a man has already fallen head over heels for you. Then he'll do just about anything to make you happy, even if there isn't really anything immediate in it for him.

Good Men Want to Take Care of Women—Let Them

As much as men seem totally disconnected from their feelings a lot of the time and overly macho, the truth is that many of them are softies at heart. They want to take care of us as much as we want to take care of them.

If a man that you like and trust offers help, take it. It makes him feel important and significant. Though I fully believe in the idea of woman's empowerment, which says that we women can do things for ourselves (which we can), I also understand that men don't like to feel useless. They want to feel needed. So if one of your goals is to have a happy, long-term relationship with a man, you have to recognize both his needs AND yours and possibly make a few compromises (and vice versa of course, a relationship is a give and take).

Also, do not give a man more credit than is due for doing what men are *supposed to do*. For instance, opening a door for a lady, paying for a dinner that he asked you to, taking care of his kids or having a job—those are not exceptional acts. Those are the basic responsibilities of a man. Some women make the mistake of getting too excited about a man for doing what he's supposed to do. Some women are too quick to assume that he is "the one," when in fact he's just doing the minimum of what he's *supposed* to do. Hold men to a higher standard than that.

Understand that Men Have Types

Some women falsely assume that all men will find them attractive, but that is simply not the case. Each man has his own idea of what a physically beautiful woman is, overweight, thick or skinny, dark-skinned or pale, long hair or short hair—it is all different depending on the guy.

So don't feel like you are ugly just because one guy doesn't feel that you meet his standard of a "looker." That just means you're not that particular guy's cup of tea, but to another guy you are probably the most gorgeous woman walking. Don't allow one guy's opinion of your looks affect your overall self-esteem.

Date a Man Who Finds YOUR Look Beautiful
When dating, don't waste your time on men who don't find you that attractive, especially if their idea of attractiveness is something that you can't change without surgery, like your height or the shape of your body parts. For instance, if a man is obsessed with dating women with a certain skin tone and you do not have that skin tone, don't rack your brain trying to figure out how to attract this person. Date men who are attracted to how you look naturally.

If you start off with a man who honestly thinks YOU are physically beautiful and attractive, just as you are, you are starting off on the right foot.
How Do You Know If a Man Finds You Beautiful?
You may wonder how you will know if you're a man's type and he finds you beautiful. Well of course the first sign is that he tells you so. But you should always rely more on a man's actions than his words. Here are a few more reliable signs:

- ♥ - you catch him stealing smiley glances at you
- ♥ - he is eager to introduce you to his family or friends (wants everyone to see the woman he has)
- ♥ - his eyes are glued to you, even in a room full of other beautiful women
- ♥ - he immediately grabs your hand when around other men (he believes that you are so attractive that other guys will be looking)

Guys Like to Feel Special, Just Like We Do

Playing hard to get sometimes works, but you have to learn how to "finesse" men and make them feel important from time to time. When you learn this art, you will grab his interest and affection a lot quicker than if you stick your nose up in the air all of the time, pretending that he isn't that important to you.

I certainly do not advocate running after a man desperately, flirting too much and trying to get him to like you. But you do have to put in a little work if you want to get his full attention and affection early on. Flirting is an art—there is a way to do it while keeping firm boundaries. For instance, you want to flirt a little when texting but don't let it turn into sexting.

Once in a while, text the guy you're dating to say hi and tell him that he's been on your mind (only if it's true of course). Guys love that. They want to hear that you like them, and think about them, just like you do. Throw him a compliment once in a while, like "I really like how passionate you are when you talk about your job." Or "I love a man who isn't afraid to get his hands dirty" or whatever applies. This should be reciprocal—if he's not bothering to ever text or call you with compliments or just to say "I was thinking about you," you shouldn't be going out of your way for him.

Now some guys take these flirts a bit too far and think it is an invitation to start sexting or talking about sex. Put the guy in check immediately if that happens, while keeping the conversation light-hearted. For instance, "Hey hey, let's not get carried away" or "I see you're going into R-rated territory and we need to keep it PG, okay buddy." Don't be afraid to be firm, speak your mind and say NO (keep reading to learn about my petulant child theory and the power of NO)—most guys secretly appreciate it when you set firm boundaries.

Men Like Confident Women

I'll expand on this more in later sections, but it is an important point that you need accept.

Men like confident women, just like you want a confident man. They do not want to be with a woman who has low self-esteem and doesn't believe in herself. If you don't even believe in your own beauty and self-worth, why should anyone else?

You're probably too busy looking at celebrities and magazines and comparing yourself to those images instead of embracing your own unique beauty (see Chapter 10: Childhood and Media Brainwashing). Instead of feeling bad about not resembling celebrities you should be learning to love your own face, your own body and your own essence. You teach others how to treat you. When you hold your head high and believe in your own beauty, others have no choice but to eventually believe in it as well.

Keepin' 'Em on Their Toes

Some guys are low maintenance, others you have to keep on their toes to keep them interested. Some men get bored very easily, which is why they often cheat or lose interest in a relationship.

Keeping a man on his toes means that he is constantly wondering about you, wondering if you are actually his woman, wondering if you're actually interested in him and wondering if you're happy or unhappy with him. You're unpredictable and he looks forward to seeing what you'll do next. When a man knows without a doubt that you're hooked on him and that there's no chance that you'll ever leave him, that's when he may start to lose interest in the relationship. Keep this in mind as you progress in the dating process.

At the same time, you have to think about whether it is really worth your time and effort to constantly "entertain" a guy that you're dating in order to keep him interested. You may just want to toss him back and move onto someone who doesn't require that much maintenance.

What Makes a Guy Fall for A Woman?

The answer to this question differs from guy to guy. But in my experience it starts with the top two of that hierarchy of priorities (physical attractiveness), which draws them in and ends with the sudden realization that you are more than just a pretty face or a sexy body. If the relationship doesn't progress past the first stage of appreciating your physical attractiveness, it's unlikely that a man will develop a real bond with you at some point. He will just have some fun and eventually move on.

I have had three men in my life admit to me that they were in love with me. In two out of the three cases the relationship started with mostly physical intentions and in the third case it started off as a relationship of convenience. All ended with these guys somehow learning that I was the type of woman they wanted in their lives for the long run. They saw me as a lover, friend and someone who would support their dreams.

The bottom line is that these men eventually got to know me intimately as a person, my personality, my humor, my dedication, my heart, how hardworking I was, etc., and that is what eventually led them to fall in love with me.

It takes a lot of time for a man to get there though. They do not develop an emotional bond to a woman through sex the way that women do. So if you've been dating a guy for two months and wonder why he doesn't love you yet, you are being unrealistic. I am a firm believer that if two people invest enough time in each other, they will eventually either fall in love romantically or develop a love bond as friends.

He Drops it and You Pick It Up

Let me ask you a simple question that may seem silly.

Picture this in your head. The guy you're dating is standing right in front of you. He drops something in front of you, like his keys or wallet. Would you rush to bend over and pick it up for him? Again, this may seem a silly question, but it is actually really important because it shows your mentality as a woman.

If you will rush to fix his mistake, you might be an enabler and too eager to please.

If a man were to drop something in front of you. Let him pick it up. Let him get it. He's an able-bodied grown man.

Men "drop stuff" on women all the time in different ways. It's a test to see what type of woman you are and could set the tone for the rest of your relationship (if you even have one).

For example, if you start living with a guy he might drop his underwear in the middle of a floor and expect you to pick them up. Unless you want to pick up dirty stained drawers for the rest of your time together, your best course of action is to immediately tell him that he left his dirty underwear on the floor and to please put them in the hamper. You might not have a problem washing the clothes, but you're not going to gather them from the floor too like a maid. Be logical with him.

Another example: he drops his problems on you all of the time (your problems are never a concern of course). He's in a jam and really needs $3,000 to get out of it. Women fall for this type of thing all the time and end up on judge shows telling their tales of being used. You don't have to be cold, but don't let a man you've just met immediately start dumping all of his problems on your lap and expecting you to help solve them. He needs to handle them just like any other grown adult. The first time he does it, you can listen, but don't play the mommy role wanting to solve all of his problems and kiss his boo boos. If you do it will never stop. If he asks for it, maybe a little friendly advice, but never money or an offer to fix it for him. Remember you are not his wife and not even his girl-friend at that point.

Momma's boys have had a woman picking up after them for many years (their mommas)—that is why they are spoiled and often make undesirable partners. Women just shouldn't do that for men, men should be held responsible to pick up after themselves.

So if you are the type of woman who will rush to pick up after a guy's mistakes, you have to change your mentality. He is a man—let him be a man.

Men Today Have Too Many Choices

You may wonder why men have such a hard time set-tling on one woman, compared to men of the past.

It's simple. They have too many choices!

Have you ever been in a store to pick up a specific item and been faced with an aisle full of choices? How long did you spend in front of that aisle trying to decide? Probably a lot longer than if there were just two choices to pick from.

Well that's what's going on in the minds of many men today—they have a bevvy of choices (or at least they THINK they do) that all seem the same so they take their sweet time deciding.

One thing I have learned in my years of dating is that when you set yourself apart, and have the right mindset as well as high self-esteem, self-confidence and self-respect, men will immediately flock to you leaving the rest of their many choices in the dust.

Key Takeaways

- 💜 Good men like taking care of women—let them
- 💜 Men have types—respect that and don't feel bad about it
- 💜 Guys like to feel special and be complimented from time to time, just like we do
- 💜 Men prefer confident women who keep them on their toes
- 💜 A guy will fall for a woman when he has a chance to get to know her behind her looks and sexual attractiveness
- 💜 Let a man be a man and pick up after himself (literally and figuratively)

CHAPTER 5

How to Date Better

$\mathcal{N}$ ow that you have a bit more of an understanding of how men think, operate and make choices when it comes to women, you need to apply that knowledge to your dating habits. First, examine the hierarchy of men's needs that I wrote at the beginning of this book again:

A Man's Hierarchy of Desires/Needs in a Woman
A Looker
A Lover
A Supporter Who Believes in Him
A Friend and Confidant

If a man asks you out on a proper date, in most cases that means that you at the very least meet his idea of beauty (a Looker), however in some cases you may not be his ideal of a "looker," but he is still interested in pursuing you to get the second priority on his list—sex (a Lover)...

The Cheap Prostitute

This section might ruffle your feathers a little, but you need to hear it. You must learn to think critically and logically when dealing with men. They are very logical thinkers while women tend to act more on feelings and emotions.

(**Important note:** Just because one guy doesn't find you attractive doesn't mean that you're not. You have to stop letting the opinions and views of others define you. Confidence is key.)

If you don't meet a man's initial standard for a "Looker" (top of his list of priorities) but he still contacts you for to date, you may be up for the role of a "cheap prostitute" in his mind. Think about it—taking a woman out on a date or two before getting sex is much cheaper than paying a professional prostitute for sex.

Why do you think certain men will ask you out to drinks for a first date rather than out to dinner or something special?

Because getting you drunk is a relatively cheap and effective way to speed along the process of him getting sex from you. The truth is that he probably doesn't think you meet his ideal of a looker—at least not enough to pursue a serious relationship. So he wants to try using you as a friends with benefits instead. It's a hard pill to swallow, but you need to understand what is going on to avoid getting hurt and played time and time again. * *In some cases a guy will ask you out for one drink initially to chat and see if you click, then suggest a meal on the same date if you like each other. I don't see a problem with that.*

Now a professional prostitute charges something like $200+ an hour.

Drinks at a midscale bar for two people might run him $50 - $70 and then depending on your level of desperation he can have you for as long as he wants after that—even multiple occasions of late night booty calls without having to make any further investments in wooing you. Some guys get away with just paying $5 for a coffee date!

So how do you combat this form of "cheap prostitution?" **You simply say NO.**

You don't even have to say no to the date offer itself— just say no to the sex.

If you say no to sex after the first or second date and he continues to pursue you, this begins to change the game because he's forced to get to know you as an *actual person*. Eventually, that first item on the list (looker) starts to become less important, while the second item (lover) is being put on the backburner for now (yet still an enticing goal), and he is forced to begin looking at the real you as a person (supporter and friend). If he finds out that you are a good, supportive, confident woman and potentially a real friend in life, it'll be harder to just "pump and dump" you when and if sex does happen in the future. That is because feelings and closeness have had a chance to develop.

So just keep in mind that a guy may be hoping that you will play the role of a cheap prostitute. When you think about it this way, it becomes a lot easier to say NO to sex too soon.

Another way to think about it: don't give the guy a seedy story to tell his buddies, because that's exactly what they do when they have sex with you too soon.

When He Asks to Cuddle

If a man asks you to his house and to "cuddle" on the first "date," this is the ultimate slap in the face to your womanhood. That is because he is not even trying to invest anything for your time or make any effort to woo you at all. He wants to treat you like a prostitute without even paying you! Now how about that?

Go back to the list. He doesn't think that you meet his ideal of a "looker," so he wants to see if he can just jump right down to #2 for a quick roll in the hay without even having to take you out on a date. If you agree to go to this stranger's house, you have just accepted the role of a jump off a.k.a. booty call for as long as he desires your company. If you don't, that's fine with him because will most likely keep trying with other women who he doesn't think meet his beauty standards but who he believes will give him sex with no strings attached.

Why would you give this type of person the time of day? He isn't meeting any of your needs besides sex (which is low on the list of priorities for most women). He is also probably sexually irresponsible (i.e. a loose man with multiple children and possible STDs) and not safe to deal with.

Is it worth giving a man who does not value your unique beauty and qualities that kind of power for nothing in return but his occasional "cuddling?" Don't do it. If he is really into you, he will invest the money and time into a proper dinner or creative date where you can talk and get to know each other.

To summarize, if he hasn't fully bought into your beauty and charm by the time you move onto number two on his hierarchy of needs/desires (sex) he will probably take what he wants and then leave quickly—even if the sex is pretty good. Some men are so obsessed with looks to the point where they will even forgo sex in search of their ideal of beauty. They will even get with a husk of a woman, with little to no morals, who doesn't support him or care about his feelings just because she is very beautiful in his eyes (a trophy).

So What Should You Do to Date More Productively?

It's pretty easy. When dating you must get to know a man really well before being intimate with him. You need to experience things together. You should be friendly and feel comfortable around each other.

You should have formed some type of bond first.

If he keeps calling you for dates that means he's interested in you, so keep going on them for as long as YOU are interested. No sex.

One day he's going to be faced with a decision, commit or get off the pot. If he decides he wants to commit, and you do too, only then does sex possibly come into the picture. If he decides to move on because he can't wait, you two weren't compatible and he wasn't worth giving away your precious treasure. After some time, you might even decide that HE doesn't meet YOUR hierarchy of needs. In that case sex should have never happened.

Let me be perfectly crystal clear. Say a man is moderately attracted to you physically. If you haven't developed a bond with him yet, showing that you are the type of woman he needs in his life but you still go ahead and have sex with him, he is probably going to drop you soon after you have sex. It sounds harsh, but you are no longer of much use to him. He might get sex from you a few more times if he's bored, but his mind is already on conquering new territory (just about every man thinks he's deserving of a runway model).

Isn't this the usual scenario that plays out for women when dating?

Compare dating a man to managing a petulant child: if you give in too quickly it doesn't make the child love you anymore than he already does. It makes the child lose respect for you and begin walking over you whenever he wants something. It creates a toxic, one-sided relationship.

The woman that he finds extremely beautiful, sexy and charming (whether artificial or real) could have sex with him the very first night they meet and he will still want her—especially if she's confident, a little bitchy and demanding (more on that later). These women know a man's hierarchy and use that knowledge to their benefit, so they will do whatever possible to meet or exceed the standard of beauty, even if that means getting fake breasts, hair extensions, butt injections, liposuction, plastic surgery and tanning. They put on the charm and dress scantily to immediately attract plenty of male attention, and when they have it they use it to their full advantage.

Karma catches up to these women eventually, because looks eventually fade and even fake body parts will start sagging. If they haven't learned to develop traits beyond their looks, then they don't have much to fall back on when they reach a certain age. These women usually become bitter and angry, with only their memories of being "hot and sexy" to hold onto.

BUT you can learn a thing or two from these beautiful bitchy women—for one, stop putting the needs and wants of a man before your own. It's ok to demand what you want from a man, whether it is attention, consideration, respect, a proper date or more. You deserve to be happy too. The second thing that these women understand is that there are plenty of fish in the sea. They have no problem dating several different men at once and are unapologetic about it.

If you decide that you want to keep pursuing a man who you know is only mildly attracted to you (not recommended) then fine, but you had better not have sex with him until he expresses a serious interest in being your exclusive boyfriend. Not a moment sooner. Otherwise, be prepared to either be used for a quick romp or used as a "friend with benefits" until someone else comes along.

What Having a Bond Means

I feel the need to clarify what I mean when I say that you should have a bond with a man before sleeping with him.

What it Doesn't Have to Mean
- ♥ you watch sports and kick it together like one of the guys
- ♥ you know every single intimate detail of each others' lives
- ♥ you see each other every day and talk on the phone all night long
- ♥ you go to the spa together, blah blah blah

What it Does Mean
- ♥ you know a thing or two about his parents and siblings
- ♥ you know if he gets along with his mother or not (a crucial detail that I discuss more in a later section)
- ♥ you know where he works, what he does and if he enjoys it
- ♥ he has opened up to tell you something private about himself, such as a childhood story
- ♥ you feel comfortable talking to each other about even the most mundane topics
- ♥ you have a texting session/talk on the phone at least a few times per week (preferably one contact every day)
- ♥ you cross each other's minds at least once each day

💜 you know each other's last names and backgrounds
💜 you know each other's hopes and dreams

As you can see, when I say that you should have developed a bond with a man before having sex, I'm only saying that you should know more about him than what's on the surface. You should have a certain level of comfort with him.

If he leaves you alone because you said no to sex too soon, he's a dusty "rock" (see chapter 8) and you probably shouldn't have wasted your time with him in the first place. Be thankful you're free of that dude before he had a chance to use and hurt you.

Sorry, Texting Isn't Enough

Modern technology has made getting to know someone even harder. In the past, we would pick up the phone, call the other person and sometimes talk for hours over the phone. We would meet up more, even just to hang out at a public place, and eventually meet each other's friends or families. Bonds formed faster that way.

Nowadays women and men barely even talk on the phone in between sporadic dates. You just send text or Facebook messages here and there. Very little to no bond has formed, so invites to family barbecues on the Fourth of July and group dinners with the friends aren't as frequent.

Think about it: how can you really get to know someone through a text message here and there? How is a bond being formed? You need to hear someone's voice on a regular basis, note the inflection in his tone when he makes certain comments, laugh together, talk about the day and let him hear you sweetly say "good night" before you hang up the phone.

So the irony of the quick and fast nature of the Internet and cellphones is that is takes MUCH longer to get to know someone that you're interested in.

Ask the guy you're dating to pick up his phone and call you, or call him. If he can't do that, or when he does you can't even hold a normal conversation with him, he's probably not the guy for you. Communication is key—the more effortless it is, the better.

Make it a point to talk to the guys you're dating on the phone at least once or twice per week. This may seem like a chore at first, but you'll find that it accelerates the "getting to know you" process by leaps and bounds

On His "Best Behavior"

I was taught that a man is always on his best behavior when you first meet. His main goal is sex, so he will say all of the right things to get it. You can't possibly know his full story after just a week or a month. Take more time to get to know him before sleeping with him—if you want the relationship to be serious at some point, you must get a clear communication from him that he is interested in you as more than just a "friend with benefits," a booty call or a potential "pump and dump" victim.

And of course, you may discover that he isn't really a catch after all. In that case, keep your goodies in your pocket, toss the rock and move on.

Lukewarm is Not Enough

Though it is possible to lock it down with a man who is only mildly attracted to you at first, you probably shouldn't waste your time. If a man is just lukewarm toward you, it probably isn't worth going forward. Any time you are more into a guy than he is into you, chances are that you will end up getting hurt. If you continue to pursue a lukewarm guy and give up sex before you two develop a bond, be prepared for a prompt ghosting. As soon as he gets sex he is going to disappear faster than Casper.

How do you know a guy is lukewarm about you?

1. He doesn't respond promptly to your emails or messages

2. He is short or curt with you when having a conversation or doesn't want to talk to you on the phone
3. He breaks plans with you often (you're not a priority when something else comes up) or shows up to dates very late unapologetically
4. Goes days without contacting you (a man who is interested in you will think about you at least once a day)

These are all signs that he is lukewarm when it comes to you -- he could take you or leave you.

Cease communication with lukewarm guy and keep dating other people. He thinks you are a desperate sap that he can come tap for honey whenever he wants. Dump him now before he does it to you. You deserve better.

Stop Being So Nice and Well-Behaved All of the Time

While I don't advocate that any decent woman follow in the footsteps of bad girls who use men for money and material things, I do believe that you shouldn't be too nice when it comes to men. Most men do not like meek, quiet, reserved women (I have heard this from the horse's mouth, many times)—men like a woman who speaks up for herself. A man needs a woman who will keep him in line, not allow him to run roughshod all over her.

If a guy you are dating does something you don't like, don't be afraid to tell him so ASAP. If you're worried that he'll dump you if you speak up for yourself, therein lies the problem. You are insecure and weak if you allow a man to repeatedly do things that you don't like for fear that he won't like you anymore if you speak up for yourself. It will only get worse and worse until he gets bored with you.

I once was in a long-term relationship with a man who would come in and go out of the house at all hours, come home drunk and pretty much do whatever he wanted. I didn't want to be looked at as a bitchy girlfriend so I didn't protest much at first. When I finally had enough, I just left him. After that, I started to talk to him any way I wanted when he called or texted, as I was no longer interested in him romantically. I didn't care what he thought about me anymore. He asked me why I wasn't like that with him when we were together, because it turned him on! He couldn't get enough of me and started to go out of his way to make me happy. Go figure.

Have you ever seen a long-time happily married couple? What is usually the case? The woman is a bit overbearing and more vocal while the man is quiet and only wants to keep her happy ("yes dear").

I don't think you should be a raving bitch to a man,

but you can't be afraid to set your foot down when it's necessary.

Speak Up for Yourself... Because Men Don't Understand Silence
As an extension of the last point, it's very important to open your mouth and say something when you're unhappy about something. Don't cross your arms and pout your lips waiting for a guy to understand why you're mad. Men do not understand when we are silently angry. They don't take cues and signs as quickly as women do.

So if something bothers you, let it be known (in a respectful and calm manner of course). Talk it out and tell him what needs to change if you are to keep dating. If he can't comply and the issue is very important to you, then you may have to just toss him. Keep your options open.

Lowering Your Standards Because You're Lonely

Whenever you lower your standards just to be in some type of a relationship with a man, you are not doing yourself any favors. In fact you are doing yourself a great disservice.

People in general make the silliest mistakes when they are lonely and feeling alone. They will allow just about anyone into their lives in order to cure that loneliness.

But when you do this, you might invite all types of drama into your life that you will soon regret. What you thought was a blessing (having a man in your life) turns out to be a HUGE liability.

Establish a firm set of minimum standards for the type of man that you will allow into your life, and stick with it. No exceptions. Write it down on paper so that you will not forget.

Looking for Love for all the Right Reasons?
Before you open yourself to a new boyfriend, make sure that you are doing it for the right reasons. Do you want a boyfriend because you are open to having the right guy, a special companion in your life?

Or do you want a boyfriend because all your friends have one and you feel left out?

Is it just because you're lonely? Get a pet or a roommate!

Check your motivations and be careful what you wish for because you *just might get it*. When you want a boyfriend for the wrong reasons it breeds desperation and bad choices in men. Calm down, take a step back and explore the real reasons why you want a man in your life right now.

Maybe deep down you want to travel the world instead? Maybe you want to pursue a new passion that would take up 16 hours of your day. If these are your true desires, wouldn't it be a little selfish to try to introduce a serious boyfriend into the mix?

These questions shouldn't discourage you from wanting a boyfriend, but it should make you think. Maybe it's better if you cool down a bit in your love search right now. Maybe you shouldn't be so eager to have a serious boyfriend at the moment. Settling down with a good boyfriend is more of a marathon than a sprint to the finish line anyway. It takes some time.

Better to take your time now to eventually meet the right one at the right time than to rush into a relationship with an asshat who causes you to waste five years of your life, right?

And if you pursue what you really want to do in life, there's a good chance that you'll meet the guy for you in the midst of your work or adventure. A lot of people meet the love of their lives when they're not even looking.

If a girlfriend is making you feel bad about not having a boyfriend, don't spend as much time around her. Go to a Meetup event and meet some new single friends or get a new social hobby. Avoid women who are always talking about their husbands or boyfriends. Don't allow pressures from others to cause you to rush into a bad relationship—and remember: 8.5 times out of 10 your friends who brag or make you feel insecure about not having a boyfriend are not really happy in their own relationships. Their only joy is in making single people like you feel insufficient! Don't be like them—wait until it's right.

Date for Fun - Not as a Hunt for a Husband

Sometimes we ladies get a little over zealous about going on a date with a new guy that we like. You think that the date is going so well that surely you will be meeting each other's parents and living together soon.

Dating should be fun and flirty. It shouldn't be like an interview to evaluate your future husband. Even if the first date seems like a dream come true, refrain from planning the wedding in your head just yet.

Here's a bit of news: just about every first date is going to go well. The guy is on his best behavior and you don't know each other well enough to decide if you're really compatible just yet.

This is also why I say you shouldn't feel bad about dating several people at once. It's like a meet and greet—not a job interview where you have to make a tentative commitment.

So when you have a date, look at it in the proper perspective—a fun outing. The same goes for the next few dates. Only when you've developed a bond with the guy should you start taking the whole thing a little more seriously.

So What Do YOU Want?

I want you to start pondering this question:

What do you want more than anything from a relationship?

Here's the hierarchy or desires and needs that I believe heterosexual women prioritize when looking for a mate:

A Woman's Hierarchy of Desires/Needs in a Man
A Protector
A Provider
A Looker/Lover
A Friend and Confidant

Be honest, which of these things is most important for you? Are you really content with only having a man's presence and some sex once in a while (a.k.a. friends with benefits)?

Or do you want a partner, a protector, someone who will have your back when you need him, someone you can call and confide in when you're dealing with a difficult situation?

Be honest with yourself.

Keep this question in mind as you continue to read this book.

Key Takeaways

- 💜 Don't play the role of a man's "cheap prostitute"—exchanging sex for a meal or a drink.
- 💜 Don't be intimate with a man until you have formed a bond with him first.
- 💜 Say NO. Dating a man is sometimes like managing a petulant child: giving in to his demands just gives him license to walk all over you.
- 💜 Stop putting the needs and wants of a man before your own.
- 💜 Guys are always on their "best behavior" when you first meet them
- 💜 If a guy is just "lukewarm" about you, best to leave him alone.
- 💜 Quit being nice and well-behaved all of the time—most men want a woman who isn't afraid to speak up for herself.
- 💜 Don't fall into the trap of lowering your standards because you're lonely, unless you want to end up like your unhappy attached or married friends who settled.
- 💜 Date to have fun, and if something serious happens, great.

CHAPTER 6

The Various Types of Women

ℳ aybe it would help to analyze a few types of women to understand where they are going right or wrong. See where you may fall on this list.

"Homely" Women Who Always Seem to Have a Man
Besides the beautiful bad girls, there is another group of women who always seem to get the guy—women who may be considered "homely" or unattractive by traditional standards yet are always married or taken. Like the traditionally beautiful sexy girl, these women also understand men and use this understanding to get what they want.

These women usually have great personalities, they are fun to be around and aren't afraid to crack a joke once in a while (even if it is on themselves). They make good FRIENDS. These women have a very attractive trait that goes beyond looks or sex appeal—they are <u>confident</u> and secure in themselves. They care very little about what other people, including men, think about them and exude happiness. Men love that.

These women also aren't afraid to <u>ask for what they want</u>, including a commitment.

A traditionally pretty nice woman who is insecure in herself isn't long-term attractive to men. She will get "pumped and dumped" time and time again because she doesn't believe in her own woman-power and prioritizes the needs of others, especially men, before her own.

And yes in some cases the homely woman is simply offering other perks as a way to keep a man in her life, such as financial support, a place to stay, or degrading sex acts. In this case, she'll keep him around for a while but he will leave as soon as he finds a better deal. No good.

The Good, Hardworking Woman Who's Always Single
Many single women who are ignored fall into this category. They have been taught from a young age that all they have to do is be a good, nice woman in order to meet and marry a good, nice man. But unfortunately that's not how it always works anymore.

Things have changed. Men seem to be more complicated than they were in past decades. My theory is that it is due to our technologically advanced modern world—they are bombarded with so many options that they hesitate to make a choice to settle down with a good woman who would probably make them very happy for many years.

Back in the day, a man found a woman he thought was halfway attractive and nice in his neighborhood. He courted her to see if she met his needs, then they got married and had a bunch of kids. Nowadays it's much more complicated—men have online dating sites, social media, video games, HD sports and other distractions (not to mention a load of desperate women throwing themselves around freely in friends with benefits relationships).

So the "good girl" often gets overlooked. She is also more susceptible to getting used and tossed away because she is too eager to please and thinks that giving a man sex will make him love her. WRONG WRONG WRONG. She is not hip to the game, so she's constantly getting played.

She has to break out of the mentality of being "good, perfect and pleasing" and instead live bolder and more fearlessly—not just when relating with men, but in life in general!

Really Beautiful, but Still Single... Why?
If you are a woman who is considered very beautiful by societal standards but you still get "pumped and dumped" a lot, you may wonder where that all fits in this hierarchy theory. If a sexy stripper can lock down a man without fulfilling the other needs on

a man's list of priorities, why can't you rest on your beautiful features?

Well, there are a few possible reasons.

1) You rushed into sex with him shortly after meeting and it wasn't that good.
2) You have a needy, clingy energy and he can tell that you are desperate
3) You have low self-esteem despite your amazing looks or are too eager to please others

Yes, men love beautiful women, but that isn't enough in the long-term. The woman also has to be fun, charismatic, confident, sexy and a little dangerous (bad girl) in order to hold his attention.

A beautiful woman becomes very unattractive when she's insecure and needy. A homely woman can look like the Queen of the Nile when she is confident and has a great personality.

So again, if you are beautiful and think that trait alone is going to make a man fall in love you, you are sorely mistaken. Say no to quick sex until he has a chance to learn more about you and peel back your layers if you are more of a reserved or insecure personality. Don't be afraid to come out of your shell and do not become too attached to one guy too soon. Date and have (safe and smart) fun.

Women with High Sexual Energy
We all have different energies that we give off to others. A woman who gives off very hot and steamy sexual energies to men needs to be very careful when dating.

I have come to a place where I have to admit that I am one of these women. Unconsciously I give off high sexual energy. It's no wonder that so many guys from my past wanted to rush into sex with me as quickly as possible after meeting me. I can admit that in the past I was one of those mild-mannered, insecure women who was too eager to please, so looks and sex alone wasn't enough to keep most of those guys around.

Sex is never enough when it comes to building a healthy, long-term relationship with a man. If you are one of those women who give off strong sexual energy, tone it down a bit. Dress nice but not too sexy on your first date. Put the cleavage away so that he will spend more time looking at your eyes than your boobs. Wait until you two are official and bonded in a relationship to pull out those really sexy dresses and tight hot pants once in a while. Also, never go on a date if you are feeling sexually charged (i.e. horny). If need be, release that energy (if you catch the drift) before your date so that you won't jump into anything stupid too soon.

Don't go over a guy's house too soon if you have a high sexual energy. Don't even play around like that.

You will have a very hard time resisting the lure of time alone with him—especially if drinks are involved. Also avoid deep kissing early on in the dating process.

CHAPTER 7

Change Your Perspective: What Do YOU Want?

*D*ating better also requires you to change your mindset and perspective when it comes to men. You have to get out of the mode of going out of your way to please men and start going out of the way to please yourself more. **You need to be happy first and foremost.**

YOU ARE THE PRIZE to be won over, not the guy. Understand and accept that as the truth. Say it to yourself each morning when you look in the mirror.

Think About Your Needs
The woman's hierarchy of needs is protector, provider, lover, friend or some variation of that order.

So think about this: if a man hasn't proven that he can offer at least one of the first two priorities on this list (protector or provider) why are you even giving him the time of day? Why are you continuing to talk to him?

Why are you so willing to give up SEX to a man who hasn't proven himself to be a protector, provider or friend to you?

Desperation, that's why.

Nice women are so desperate for approval that they will compromise their own values and needs to meet someone else's. TIME TO WAKE UP FROM THAT NIGHTMARE!

Your values, motivations, needs and desires are more important than a stranger's! I would even extend that to say that your values, motivations, needs and desires are more important than anyone else's (with the exception of children because they didn't ask to be here).

A lot of women don't really think of themselves as a prize—they think the man is the prize. That is backwards thinking that not only destroys self-esteem but also disrupts the social order between men and women. If you don't agree, think about how things worked in the past. A man came to a woman's house to court her, win her over and ask her father for her hand in marriage. That resulted in plenty of marriages and long-term relationships. Nowadays, women think they have to go after men, convince him to want to date her (sometimes even pay for the dates) and then convince HIM that she's worthy of being his girlfriend. You can see the results of that approach: plenty of short-term hookups, breakups and divorces.

If you can get to a point where you start to think of yourself as a prize and prioritize your own needs, the world begins to open up to you. That needy, ugly emotion called desperation keeps good people and opportunities from flocking your way. Have confidence in yourself and put your needs first. You matter!

The Difference Between Being Confident and Being Controlling

A lot of women confuse confidence with controlling behavior. Men do not like to be controlled under an iron fist -- they like to feel as if they are in control of themselves and the boss of their families even if that's not the full truth.

Confident women are attractive. Controlling women are just scary, annoying and abrasive. The difference is this: confident women set rules for themselves while controlling women try to set rules for everyone else.

A man has the freedom to CHOOSE if he will go along with the rules that a confident woman sets for herself, but with a controlling woman he doesn't have much of a say in anything. It's almost like being in slavery (that's where they get the term "ball and chain").

Ask any HAPPILY married woman (not just married, but HAPPILY married) -- she has an unspoken rule over her household but knows how to make her man feel important. She sets rules for herself and what type of conditions she will live in, but doesn't FORCE them on her spouse. He can choose not to comply if he wants, but there is no guarantee that she'll stick around or be happy about it. It's totally up to him.

Simply put, confidence is not the same as arrogance, selfishness or controlling behavior. Controlling behavior might work for a short while on weak-minded men, but a decent guy is not having any of it. Weak-minded men might stick around for a while out of fear, but soon enough they're quietly plotting ways to escape.

Make Him Earn You
Men place value on things that they've earned. Make him work for you (the prize) and all that comes with winning that prize.

He must care for you as a person (not a sex toy) before you have sex with him if you want the relationship to progress to something meaningful.

SEX is too easy. Becoming a man's friend is a real challenge that requires time and work (for both people).

Don't Go to Him, Let Him Come to You

If you agree to go on a date, don't agree to meet at a place close to where he lives, especially if it's out of your way. It is a set up for getting you back to his place for sex. One of the *48 Laws of Power* (a book by Robert Greene that I strongly suggest for any young single woman who feels powerless) even expresses this concept: "Make other people come to you; use bait if necessary."

Knowing this important power principle, I decided to purposely break it to test my theory for the purpose of this book. I guess you could call it an experimental date.

A guy I met online asked me out to a date at a bar/restaurant in his neighborhood. I lived about 20 minutes away at the time. I agreed because the restaurant looked interesting and it was downtown.

As soon as I arrived I could immediately sense his arrogance. He sat back trying to look as aloof as possible. He didn't even bother to stand up, pull out my chair or give me a friendly hug. He just sat there. Shortly after we began talking I knew I wasn't interested in dating him—he was a me-me-me, douchey type. He refused to buy anything to eat, claiming that he was between jobs, and didn't have a lot of money, which are very poor manners when you invite someone out for a date. I ordered something to eat anyway, knowing what was going on and smiling to myself.

At the end of the date, I pulled out my card after he examined the bill (he took his sweet time picking it up) because I already knew that he was not gentleman enough to pay the entire bill. I suggested that we split the bill. After paying, I was eager for him to leave so that I could enjoy the nice bar by myself. Toodle-oo!

Well my prediction was right—douchey dude then had the nerve to ask me up to his apartment after that! Because I agreed to go to his part of the town for our date, I guess this particular person took it to mean that I was eager and desperate enough to pay my own tab for a date he asked me on AND then give him quick sex.

I promptly declined and sent him on his way. I could see all of his arrogance deflate at that moment; he really assumed that I was desperate enough to fall for his little plan.

And unfortunately some women do. Remember what I said in chapter 5 about how some guys will try to treat you like a cheap prostitute? Well this guy actually thought he was getting some for doing and giving absolutely nothing.

The moral of the story here is, when dating early on, do not go to his turf, either make him come to your turf or meet somewhere in the middle. Make him do some work. Let him come to you. Keep in mind that if he invites you somewhere close to where he lives he is trying to set you up for a "wham bam thank you ma'am" session at his place right after.

Your Sex Is Not Irresistible

If you think that performing over-the-top sexual favors for a man the first time that you are intimate is the way to make him want to be your boyfriend, you are confused. Let's be clearer—if you think that giving an amazing blowjob to a man on the first date is the way to his heart, you are completely lost. He might call you for more blowjobs, but not to go meet his family anytime soon.

It doesn't matter how magical you think your lady parts are, they're just not. Women who do successfully use their sex to get what they want are cold and calculating—they have it down to a science. They are shameless. They are not nice and do not care about love. They know men inside out and exploit this knowledge. They study this stuff. You do not, at least at this moment, so quit trying to use your sex alone to get a boyfriend. It's demoralizing and only makes you look desperate.

Yes I'm Dating Other Guys, And?

Men can be a peculiar bunch at times. They are very possessive yet at the same time very afraid of commitment. One minute he'll tell you he's not really ready for a relationship, but as soon as he learns that another guy's checking you out he scrambles to lock it down with you.

Yet for some reason, so many of us women are still hesitant to admit that we're still seeing other guys when asked. You may fear that he'll want to stop dating you or assume that you're loose, but in fact the opposite is true—he'll probably want to date you even more than before and try to claim you as his.

So here's a tip... if he asks you if you are dating other guys and you do not have a commitment with him then tell him the truth: **YES** you are dating other guys. It is okay to admit this, if it is true of course. It will awaken a competitive spirit in him that could eventually lead to you getting *exactly* what you want from him. When you admit that you are dating other people, he knows that he does not have you locked down. It also shows him that you are desirable to other men. A man who is interested in you even mildly will then start to go out of his way to convince you that he's the one for you and not that other guy. It's something straight out of the Animal Kingdom.

I have experienced this firsthand, many times. In one case, when an ex-boyfriend started calling me out of the blue, the new guy that I was dating learned about this and immediately became jealous and competitive. Instead of writing me off, he worked harder to make me his exclusive girlfriend.

The Art of "No"

If you want to be taken seriously as a woman, by anyone in your life, you have to learn to say "no." And there is an art to it.

I know it's probably a little hard for you to say no, with those nice girl sensibilities that you learned as a young child, but it is really easy once you get the hang of it.

You must tell men "no" so that they learn boundaries. It is similar to checking a child—"No! You can't have that, so stop asking!" The child may cry and get upset for a while, but eventually he'll be alright. And over time he'll learn to respect you as a woman who isn't going to let him have his way all of the time.

The most important "no" that you must tell a man that you've just started dating is "no" to having sex too soon. The request for sex usually comes under some other pretense, like "why don't you come over to watch a movie?" or "why don't we cuddle?" Don't be mistaken, these are invitations for sex. Say no to them all until you are comfortable and secure with your relationship with this guy.

As I said before, there is an art to saying no.

You don't have to be blunt and nasty about it; add some finesse and wit whenever possible. A few simple ways to decline a man's invitations:

- ♥ I really have to wash my hair (classic, you have "better" things to do)
- ♥ No thanks, I'd rather cuddle up with my book tonight!
- ♥ I'm not really in the mood for watching a "guy flick," tonight,
- ♥ Sorry, but no, it's past my bedtime (yawn)

You get the idea. Make it a game: experiment with creative and witty ways of telling a guy no when he asks you to do something that you don't want to do or that you're not completely comfortable with at the time.

Stop Taking Men Who Haven't Proven Themselves Yet So Seriously

The main reason why so many of us ladies get hurt time and time again is that we just care too much about what men think—even the ones who haven't even proven themselves to be an actual catch yet!

Think about the last guy that you went out on a date with. Was he really "all of that?" Was he your dream guy? Or was he just another regular guy that you could meet anywhere?

If he was a regular guy, why were you so pressed to impress him? Why did you take the date with him so seriously that you got dressed to the nines, got your nails and hair done and thought about the date all day?

How many times have you gone all out for a date—shopping, hair, nails, waxing and everything just to show up and see that he has barely managed to pull on a t-shirt with dirty jeans?

First off, this is an offense that I almost see as grounds for immediate termination. You might just want to cut the date short. If he can't even throw on a nice button-down shirt and clean pants for your date he probably doesn't value your company or time that much.

But even more important is this question: even if he had the potential to be your dream guy, why did you look at the first date like you had to impress HIM? When dating, you should be fully confident in the idea that you are HIS dream date. He is vying for the position of YOUR boyfriend. He should be trying to impress YOU.

Stop taking every man so seriously in the first place. They are just fellow human beings, not magical oracles. Your future does not hang in the balance because of one simple date. If it's right, it's right no matter what you do, say or look like. If it doesn't work out, toss the rock (see chapter 8) and move on.

If it progresses, go with it and continue to maintain your confident aloofness at the whole thing until it becomes the real thing.

Controlling Your Emotions

You may wonder if it is possible to control the effects of that chemical (oxytocin) that gets released when you do decide to have intimate relations with a man.

Well the first way to control it is to recognize that it exists, and now you do (see chapter 1). You can rest assured that it's partially a biological reaction. He's not really "all that." Now that you recognize this, you can laugh about it and eventually release those insecure feelings that are driving you crazy.

Do the following:
- 💜 laugh about it all
- 💜 relax and release the negative energy
- 💜 evaluate the situation (is it worth being upset about this guy?)
- 💜 take the appropriate action

So after you have laughed and released, evaluate what has been going on since you were intimate with this guy. If he called you the next day trying to figure out when he could see you again, no need to stress. If you're still interested in him, just proceed. If he hasn't called you for a week since you were intimate, there's a problem. Instead of dwelling on it, chalk this up to a mistake, laugh about it, delete his number, move on and keep dating. Next time, be a lot smarter about who you give your treasure.

And always use protection!

Once you do move on, do not allow him back because then you risk getting thrown into that dreaded FWB zone. You will eventually get hurt. Let's be clear, if a guy has sex with you and lets days or weeks go by before calling you again, he's an inconsiderate jerk and he's just not that into you. When you suddenly texts you out of the blue months later, it's because you are a last option or he just broke up with someone else. Toss that rock way out into the sea and just take this as a learning experience. It doesn't mean that there's something wrong with you, just in your choice of a guy.

When You Really *Do* Just Want Sex

There are certain times in a woman's life when she honestly only wants sex (or at least she has convinced herself of that). I don't recommend it, but if you do decide that you only want a sex-only relationship, it's imperative that it's safe and that you follow your intuition. You simply can't fall for the guy, but if you do, then you'll see that the words in this guide ring true.

When you're ready for a serious relationship that will pass the test of time, you'll have to let go of that sex-only mentality.

So What Do YOU Want?

I asked this question earlier in the book, and I'm going to ask it again now.

What do you want more than anything from a relationship?

A Woman's Hierarchy of Desires/Needs in a Man

A Protector

A Provider

A Looker/Lover

A Friend and Confidant

Be honest, which of these things is most important for you? Are you really content with only having a man's presence and some sex once in a while (a.k.a. friends with benefits)?

Or do you want a partner, a protector, someone who will have your back when you need him, someone you can call and confide in when you're dealing with a difficult situation?

Keep pondering this as you continue to read this book.

Key Takeaways:

- ♥ Put your needs first—you matter.
- ♥ You are the prize, not the guy. Start shifting to that mentality.
- ♥ Controlling women set rules for other people, confident women set rules for themselves.
- ♥ When dating, don't go to men, let them come to you (not to your place, but to a place that is convenient for YOU).
- ♥ Performing amazing sexual favors on the first date is not the way to a man's heart—just to his bed.
- ♥ Stop taking men so seriously as viable potential partners, until they give you a good reason to do so.
- ♥ Get control over your emotions to control that pesky oxytocin effect that makes you attach to men too soon.
- ♥ If you can *honestly* say that you only want sex from a man, be careful not to let your emotions get involved and use plenty of precautions to avoid unwanted outcomes.

CHAPTER 8

Picking Through a Pile of Rocks to Find a Gem

So you may say to yourself that you didn't have any idea you were dealing with a damaged goods guy, but I think that you did—you just ignored the signs.

- ♥ he was always staring at your boobs or ASSets
- ♥ he was always talking about himself rather than trying to learn more about you
- ♥ he suggested "cuddling" very early on in the relationship (that's code for "free sex")
- ♥ he didn't have a car, place or job of his own and tried to infringe on yours
- ♥ he insisted on not using condoms (now you have to raise a child solo or deal with other issues on your own)

I won't lie—dating modern men has become a bit of a chore, at least in my experience. I have a theory that something happened around the year 2000—a shift in dating dynamics. As I mentioned earlier, I think it may have something to do with the fast growth of the Internet.

I liken dating nowadays to searching through a pile of rocks to find a gem. Values and morals in this country have declined significantly over the past few decades, no doubt about it. Media influences have played a role. No longer do you have a plethora of responsible men like your father or grandfather to choose from. There are a whole lot of rocks and not as many gems to choose from.

Sort through that pile of rocks carefully. Check a few signs to quickly separate the wheat from the chaff.

If he tells you he's horny and you don't know anything about him? That's a rock, toss him.

He has five baby mamas and no job? Toss that rock over your shoulder, and quick!

All that he can talk about is his ex? That's a rock too. He's not over her yet and will run back to her as soon as she finds herself in a jam. Toss him!

Picking up a rock is like going to the store, picking up a broken or damaged product, and then wondering why it doesn't work when you get it home. You'll stare at it for a while trying to figure it out, but ultimately it will just become a paperweight, a burden, the longer you don't take it back to the store. Why buy something that's broken?

Why force a relationship with a broken man who won't work in more ways than one?

Better to be patient. Shop around until you come across a man that's just right for your needs.

This is not to say that a damaged goods man can't ever fix himself. But he's going to have to step his game up and thoroughly polish himself into a gem BEFORE you allow him into your life. This is less and less likely to happen the older he gets. Remember: it is NOT your job to "fix" or change a grown man.

More Signs That You've Encountered a "Rock"
- ♥ He has 69 or some other sexual reference in his screen name or email address. Sex is his only goal. TOSS HIM BACK
- ♥ He makes a sexual reference to you and you haven't even gone out on a date yet TOSS
- ♥ He doesn't have a job or money of his own TOSS
- ♥ He asks you out then expects you to pay for your half of the bill (or the whole bill!). Either he is too cheap or doesn't value you enough to treat you to a date. Either way, that is the very first act of disrespect, and there will be more – TOSS
- ♥ He can't look you in the eye at all TOSS
- ♥ He lies about small things TOSS
- ♥ He openly lusts over other women in your presence (he's disrespectful) TOSS

- ♥ For a first "date" he suggests coming over your house for movies and "cuddling" TOSS
- ♥ He whines and complains about women being gold diggers, bitches or hos TOSS
- ♥ He gets angry at the drop of a hat and can't manage his emotions (soon he'll be taking it out on you) TOSS
- ♥ He's always talking about himself, and never shows a genuine interest in YOUR life TOSS

The longer you keep entertaining the rocks, the more you're wasting precious time that could be better spent checking out other, much better guys (the gems) who have more potential as boyfriends.

If you're serious about having a meaningful relationship one day, don't waste a minute of your time with rocks. They are worn down by life and have the potential to hurt you really badly.

Watch out for those smooth, shiny pebbles too. They seem attractive on the surface but really you're just holding onto a good looking rock. And also be careful you're not passing up a gem who looks a little rough around the edges at first. The gem guy may not look that shiny to you at first, but if you dust him off a little you may reveal his true brilliance.

Hold onto the gems and give them a chance to prove themselves to you. Gems are guys who are realistic in their expectations of a woman—they aren't looking for a rich perfect supermodel who cooks cleans and performs acrobatics in bed. They understand that people, including themselves, are perfectly flawed and come in all sorts of packages. They can love and appreciate the right woman beyond her looks, sex or status in life. Of course these gems are hard to find, but if you concentrate on drawing that type of man into your life he will eventually show up.

Set high standards for the men in your life (instead of lowering yourself to theirs) and watch how they scramble to meet them! It's human nature.

Guys Who Don't Like Their Mothers
There is one type of rock that you should toss as soon as you identify him. The guy who absolutely hates his mother!

A man's feelings for his mother will eventually rain down on you. This is a fact—this is science! Men learn how to love women by first loving their mothers. Men who hate their mothers have a hard time loving anyone for that matter and are more prone to being abusive. There's no need to discuss this much further—just toss the rock. Do not waste your time.

But I Didn't Know He Was Bad for Me! He Seemed Great at First!
Have you ever heard a woman say this? Have you ever heard YOURSELF say this? Single mothers who have deadbeat children's fathers often say

this—the truth is that she didn't take enough time to get to know the guy before sleeping with him.

As I was taught, men are always on their "best behavior" when you first meet. They will always seem like princes for the first few dates. They will be on their best behavior right up until you have sex; then the act is over. The true him will come out, whether it is good or bad.

This is yet another reason why it's so important to have a bond with a guy before sleeping with him. You have to peel back layers and learn much more about him than what his favorite food is or what he likes to do for fun.

You should know how he interacts with his mother. You should know if he is a substance abuser. You should know what kind of friends he hangs around (are they hateful womanizers?). You should know everything possible about his previous relationships with women. If he has children, you should know how often he sees them and if he supports them. You should know if he has ever laid hands on a woman (criminal background).

Some women date men with long criminal records and don't even know it. How is he going to be an asset to your life and the life of your kids if he is in and out of jail? Here's a clue: if he can't get a regular job at a mainstream business there is likely a reason for that. Not to say that you should shun a man who has a past, but you need to know that it is firmly in his *past* and that he has a good, trustworthy character.

While I'm Over Here Picking through the Rocks, My Friends Are Getting Married...
Change your perspective. Getting married isn't that hard. In fact it's pretty easy if you're willing to lower your standards.

Women lower their standards all the time just to get married, which is why you really shouldn't envy married women. Chances are good that she picked up a rock, dusted it off and put it right in her pocket.

A lot of women will settle for a guy that they aren't that attracted to, or a guy who is in and out of prison, or a guy who is unemployed and frequently out of work. Some women will even buy their own ring just so that they can say they're a Mrs.

The question is: do you really want to be one of these women? Probably not—you are a smart, sensible woman who wants the best for herself, which is probably why you are still single and picking through those rocks. Finding a great guy who is just right for you takes time and patience. You should take your time, date and get to know the guys that you're dating before you choose one to settle down with.

Can't Say You Weren't Warned

Countless women fall victim to games and become angry and bitter at men because of it. But it's not them, it's YOU. You are allowing it to happen time and time again. Recognize the poor choices that you're making in men and then stop making them.

Maybe you should put a little less weight on those top two items on your list of needs (protection and money) for the time being and shift more focus on the third point (is he a potential friend and confidant?). Take the time to find out if the guy has the capability of caring deeply for you as a human being and friend before giving him anything that he desires.

Remember: There's No Ring On That Finger...

One mistake that I've repeatedly made when dating was to pick up a rock that I thought was a gem, stop looking and merrily skip away with that "gem" (which was actually a pretty rock) in my hand. Not long after that I'd open my hand to reveal that my palm was all cut up and dusty. The rock falls to the ground, I trip over it and land flat on my face. Going through this process hurt me so badly that I didn't even want to go back to sorting through the rock pile at all.

Do you follow the metaphor? In other words, I would find a man that I liked, settle on him too soon, and then completely stopped dating other men. Great guys would approach me, but in my mind I was already in a "relationship" so I declined their advances. Soon after I would get dumped (or have to do the dumping) and be left feeling very stupid for wasting my time.

Just because you start dating a guy you like doesn't mean you have to stop dating other guys. Date as many guys as your schedule can handle and have fun. When one meets your requirements (and you his) and you both make it official THEN you can go exclusive—not a moment sooner. If you stop dating other guys too soon you could miss out on a real gem while playing around with a rock or a pebble.

Key Takeaways:

- 💜 Learn the difference between a man who is a dusty rock with jagged edges or a brilliant gem who shines bright and will add beauty to your life.
- 💜 Hold onto a gem when you find one.
- 💜 Instead of lowering yourself for men, make men rise to your standards. The ones worth dating will scramble to meet them.
- 💜 Avoid men who hate their mothers.
- 💜 Don't allow women who grabbed "rocks" and got married to pressure you into doing the same. Wait for the right one.
- 💜 Keep dating (even if it's more than one guy) until you meet the one who meets your requirements and clearly expresses to you that he wants you in his life.

CHAPTER 9:

The Law of Attraction/Love and Dating

*I*f you're constantly having problems attracting and having successful relationships with men, you may have to look within. Sometimes it's the energy that you're giving off that is the problem. It could be a problem with your personality, a controlling attitude, a negative mindset, unattractive behaviors or an unrealistic outlook on men and relationships.

Start with this question: what is your mindset right now toward men in general?

Is it:

"I hate men, they are all assholes and users!"

Or is it closer to:

"I am surrounded by awesome men everywhere, one of them is made just for me and we'll find each other soon!"

The answer to that could play a major role in why you're having problems in relationships and why you're constantly meeting poor quality guys. The first answer says that you've been hurt by someone and you can't let the past go, so you place that negative energy on every guy that you come across, whether you realize it or not.

If you've never heard of the law of attraction, it's a good thing that you're reading this guide. It's time that you learn what it's all about.

You Attract What You Are
The law of attraction simply says that you attract what you are to yourself in life. It also says that you attract what you think about (and talk about) all day. It's also called the "law of love" because you attract more of what you LOVE to yourself all of the time.

It's pretty deep stuff, but actually very simple at the same time. If you're a negative, unhappy and angry person, all that you see and attract are negative, unhappy and angry people to you. But when you're a positive, loving person who thinks good thoughts, good people are drawn to you.

When you focus more on the things that you love, you bring more of that into your life. And when you focus more on the things and people you hate, you bring more of that into your life as well.

This law has been talked about for hundreds of years by many thinkers, rich men and women, inventors and innovators, but many people still don't get it. The law of attraction (sometimes called the law of love) is as strong and real as the law of gravity.

So keeping this new information in mind, how does that relate to your relationships and dating? Well, if you have a negative viewpoint about men and dating, chances are you are going to have negative experiences with men and meet all of the bad ones. Then they hurt you and you get even madder. It's a vicious cycle.

I visit online dating forums frequently and read what women are saying about men. A lot of them have given up on finding love and declare so publicly. They say that they hate men and all men are the same. They are sending out bad energy, and that is why they keep coming across the same bad men time and time again. The same is true for men who are constantly complaining about women being gold diggers and users. That's what they attract to themselves.

You Have to Be Focused on Your Goal

If you really want something (or someone), you need to be passionate about your goal. You can't "half-step" it. If you want a good man in your life you have to be passionately tied to the idea of having a good man in your life.

So if on one hand you're longing for a man in your life, but on the other hand you are saying "I don't need a man, I can do it all by myself!" you are being inconsistent. You are not expressing to the Universe that you are passionate about your goal, so the chances are slim that you'll attract a great guy into your life.

Women who are passionate about getting married (even if it is unfortunately for all the wrong reasons) tend to get married because they are very focused on their goal. They have a definite chief aim—they know exactly what they want and will do whatever is necessary to achieve it.

I don't think you should model your life after these women—many find themselves in unhappy marriages only because they are more focused on the act of getting married than on finding the RIGHT man for them (be careful what you wish for because you just might get it!). I just want you to understand the power of knowing exactly what you want and going after it.

Change Your Thoughts to Change Your Life

ALL men are dogs
ALL men are only out for one thing

ALL men are cheaters and abusers

No they are **NOT**. You have just been unconsciously attracting the bad ones to your doorstep for years through the law of attraction, so you think that's all that's out there.

I tell you there is GOLD in "them there" hills. Real gems. Unfortunately many gems are buried under the rocks so they don't always get their chance to shine.

It's your job to patiently toss away rocks while actively envisioning great men in your life.

The bottom line here is that you have to change your thought process when it comes to dating and men if you want better results. Stop imaging the horrible way that the last bad guy treated you and start thinking about what you actually *want* from a relationship. Meditate on it daily.

For instance, envision you and your ideal man in a big beautiful house or apartment, hugged up on each other, watching movies, laughing, kissing and enjoying each other. Imagine your children playing in an adjacent room. Imagine your man installing new cabinets in your kitchen while you watch, adoringly, with a cup of coffee in your hand.

Keep those images in your mind and focus on them every morning or whenever you have a free moment. Some experts on this subject say that a thought becomes stronger when you focus on it for at least 17 seconds. Daydream. If you keep this up (focusing on the positive things you want instead of the negative things you don't want), slowly but surely you will start to see some positive changes happen in your dating life. This also applies to other aspects of your life, by the way.

Learning to Love Yourself
"Learning to love yourself... it is the greatest love of all." Beautiful and true words sung by the late Whitney Houston, one of my favorite singers from childhood. I used to sing that song over and over as a child but the words never really sunk in until I was grown.

It sounds trite, but until you learn to love yourself fully it will be very difficult to find complete happiness and love from another. I still struggle with this to this day; that negative self-talk that says I'm not good enough or not pretty enough to be loved or not smart enough to be successful.

At one point, I had someone in my life who loved me unconditionally—he talked about me to everyone, introduced me to his closest friends and family and even put a ring on my finger. But despite all of these expressions of love, deep down, I didn't really believe him. I couldn't grasp it because my negative self-talk was so strong. I would secretly think to myself, "what in the hell is there to love about me?"

As Lisa Nichols, a transformational speaker and one of my favorite people says, "we teach people how to treat us." If you don't really love who you are, how can you realistically expect a stranger to learn to love you?

You Can't Date if You're Angry

Anger will cloud your judgment and create all types of barriers to meeting the right guy for you. In fact, it will most likely cause you to meet angry, negative men. That's what you're attracting.

Angry people are very easy to spot. A guy contacted me on an online dating site once. In his first email he asked why I was single. I told him the truth (just getting over some dramas and now back on the dating scene) then I asked him why he was single. He immediately started ranting about women and how they aren't real and not submissive to men. I immediately sensed the bad vibes—he was obviously an angry and bitter person—so I didn't respond.

He messaged me a few hours later with a snide comment, "So I guess I answered your question huh." I decided I would send him an honest message back. I told him I was looking for a guy who had positive vibes and wished him well in his search.

Needless to say, back came an angry message about how disrespectful it was to not reply to him, I'm just like everyone else, blah blah blah.

This is exactly why angry or hurt people shouldn't be dating. They are desperate to find someone to love but clouded by their anger at the same time. They perpetuate a negative cycle when they do meet someone. They are angry at the world, both women and men, so all they attract to themselves is situations and people who just make them angrier. Positive and happy people want to get as far away as possible.

If you are still angry and bitter at someone or something, do not date just yet. Clear the air. Do some soul searching and inner reflection. Meditate. Wait until you are feeling good about yourself and other people again. Wait until you have positive thoughts and beliefs about people again before you try to involve someone new in your life.

Key Takeaways:

- Your overall mindset about men has a huge impact on how you relate to them AND the ones that frequently enter into your life.

- The law of attraction is a law that governs our lives (though mostly unknown) that says you attract what you ARE, DO and THINK (dig deep to understand what that means).

- Focus in on your goal (a great relationship) if you really want it come true.

- Update your thoughts to upgrade your life – all men are NOT dogs, just the ones you may have had the misfortune of attracting.

- We teach people how to treat us—love yourself first, unconditionally, before you expect another person to love you unconditionally.

- Don't try to date until you get over your anger issues.

CHAPTER 10

Childhood and Media Brainwashing

From the time we're young girls, we're receiving suggestions from the media on how we should look, act and behave. We're told to be "good little girls." We're told that girls are "sugar and spice and everything nice." We're taught that if we're good, sweet and patient a white knight will ride in on a horse and save us. We're told that we have to fit ONE model of attractiveness, which causes many of us to feel insufficient if we don't even come close (just look at the covers of the magazines in your neighborhood grocery store).

Leave Your Fantasy World

A lot of grown women still live in this fantasy world where a white knight comes along and sweeps them off their feet. But when they reach 30, and he still hasn't come, they start to unravel.

Don't let this happen to you. The reality is that relationships take time and work—it's a give and take.

The reality is that if you wait for someone else to save you, you may be waiting for a very, very long time.

The reality is that women who *aren't* so "good and nice like sugar and spice" frequently get scooped up, married and swept off of their feet. There's no logic to it.

It's time to break out of the limiting beliefs that have been ingrained in you from childhood by your family, friends and the media. The messages telling you that you have to be "this or that" in order to be loved.

Start living your life with basic common sense, like a *grown woman* who follows her own intuition.

Your Best Is Never Enough: Quit People Pleasing

As young girls many of us are taught to be overly loving, supportive and understanding of others—especially men. As we get older, this morphs into an *obsessive compulsion* to be loving, supportive and understanding of men; even when they are complete assholes and not offering anything in return.

A top reason why you're always a FWB and never a girlfriend: you're always doing too much. You need to relax. Stop allowing that little girl brainwashing to rule your life. Time to be a grown woman—you have needs and wants too, so don't be afraid to express them. Let your needs and wants be **known**, then fold your hands behind your head (figuratively) and let the guy take care of you. If he won't even court you, toss that rock and move onto the next candidate. He's just another human being, with flaws and all, just like you.

Fear: Our #1 Enemy when Dating

If I could pinpoint one thing that causes so many people to be single, it is fear.

- 💜 Fear of rejection
- 💜 Fear of the unknown
- 💜 Fear of failure
- 💜 Fear of judgment

And for women the list of fears gets even longer.

- 💜 Fear of being used up by a man
- 💜 Fear of being labeled a ho, bitch or slut
- 💜 Fear of losing a man we like
- 💜 Fear of being hurt again

You have to let go of these fears if you want to date successfully.

Women allow potential judgments from the world, whether it be parents, siblings, friends or strangers, to determine our actions. Instead of going after what we want we focus more on achieving what other people want for us.

Start living your life with your best interests in mind. Goal: be fearless.

Key Takeaways:

- 💜 Quit people pleasing—you will never be able to please everyone, including the men you date.
- 💜 Release the limiting beliefs you've held onto since childhood.
- 💜 Live fearlessly.

CHAPTER 11

Online Dating Tips for Women

$\mathcal{T}$here are many different ways of meeting new guys, but online dating seems to be very popular now. I think it's worthwhile to talk a little about online dating.

If you aren't having much luck dating online, it's probably because your online profile is lacking. Look at your online dating profile like an advertisement. What attracts you to an advertisement? First the featured photo grabs your attention (we're all pretty visual), then you read the headline to find out what it's about, then if you're still interested you take the time to read what the "product" is all about.

So set up your online profile to draw in more of the right types of guys.

Your Photos

A lot of women make one of three mistakes when it comes to photos
💜 Posting an unflattering picture

- 💜 Posting a picture that is too flattering, fake, overly retouched or old
- 💜 Posting an overtly sexual picture

When presenting yourself online, you need to be honest while showing yourself in a positive light. Include a photo of your upper torso (fully clothed) and one of you performing some fun activity around other people. Convey an image of yourself as not only attractive but also social.

Avoid posting sexual pictures. That includes pictures of you bending over to show off your booty, deep cleavage or posing in a two-piece bathing suit. That will draw all kinds of negative attention that you don't want if you're trying to lock it down with one special gem of a man.

Headline

The headline is a feature offered by many dating sites. It asks for a quick summary of who you are, what you are about and what you're looking for in about 20 words or less. As you can imagine, this can be a difficult feat to achieve.

When writing the headline, again think of an advertisement. You want to draw in the right attention to eventually close the deal. A lot of women believe that they have to make sexual references on their profile in order to attract men. If you write something like "Party Girl Looking for Some Fun Nights," then don't be surprised when you get a bunch of guys looking for a one night stand. But if you write something authentic that is closer to what you actually want from a relationship, you'll attract more of the right attention to you.

Writing Your Story (But Not a Book)

Some people make the mistake of writing an entire novel on their online profile. Ever heard of TLDR (too long didn't read)? People have short attention spans— I think the stat is that you have about three seconds to grab a visitor's interest before he clicks away from a web page.

Not many people who just visited your online profile for the first time have the time to read a long essay about your life and interests. Keep your profile to about 100-200 words per section. Just give a light review of what you are about and what your interests are. Say something funny or humorous—making someone laugh is always a good thing. It also opens up a possible conversation and shows the world that you have a personality.

Avoid writing a long list of everything that you DON'T want in a man on your profile. When you do that, you only add a negative vibe to your presentation (see chapter 9 on the Law of Attraction and the Law of Love). Decent guys might look at this as a red flag that you are damaged goods, bitter or angry. Instead, write about what you love and want in a guy. It's okay to be firm in your language—for instance, "Gentlemen only, no exceptions" works a lot better than "Assholes need not apply!"

Chatting With Men Online

Once your picture and profile grabs the attention of a man online, he'll usually send you a message. The conversation you have with him will quickly determine if he's a rock or a potential gem. Look at the list in chapter 8 to remind yourself of what a rock is. If he's a rock, gracefully bow out of the conversation. Don't waste any time.

From my own experiences, I've noticed that a lot of men will ask you for your phone number soon after contacting you online for the first time. Personally, I'm not comfortable with this, but some women think it's okay. I think it is just another way of men collecting numbers from women to boost their egos, just like they used to do in club settings. Why would they want your phone number if they don't know anything about you yet?

TIP: I've found that chatting with a man on an instant messenger for about 15 minutes is the best way to determine if he's someone you want to pursue something further with. Some men have diarrhea of the mouth (or fingers)—they will type their truth and they can't take it back. The ones who are only out for sex from you will tell you so very quickly, either by constantly calling you "sexy," persistently asking for more pictures or just saying something outright disrespectful, like telling you what he wants to do to you in bed. Toss those rocks.

Your Conversation

Besides your profile, your conversation is another reason why you might not be having much luck dating online. The conversation needs to be interesting on both ends. Talk about something humorous that happened to you that day. Find out if he's living his dream. Ask him about some interesting hobby that he mentioned on his profile. The conversation tends to open up after that. I sometimes like to ask a guy about his last relationship, just to see if he will start complaining about women.

At the same time, be careful that you aren't the only one holding up the conversation. If all he's offering is one word replies or not asking you any questions, either he's lukewarm about you or not a very interesting person himself.

If you get to the third day of chatting with the same guy, chances are that he is interested and will probably ask to do something with you soon.

Know Your End Game

If you're dating online to meet someone for a serious relationship, be clear on that. Say so in your profile. If you have an online dating profile just to chat with guys for meaningless fun, then be clear with yourself on that and stick to that plan.

Free Vs. Paid Sites?

There is a theory that the best men are on paid dating sites while the bums and those looking for a quick hookup are on the free sites. I tend to agree with this theory but of course there are always exceptions. A man who is willing to invest money into his dating experience is probably more serious about finding "the one" whereas a man who frequents free sites is more likely to be doing so for fun and an occasional hookup. At the same time, I've met some relationship-minded gentlemen on free sites—they just don't believe in paying for the service if they don't have to.

Facebook Relationships

If you want your dating to turn into a successful long-term relationship, my advice is to keep it outside of Facebook and other public social platforms as much as possible. It's not uncommon to meet someone on popular social media sites, but do not post about him or chart your journey here. Facebook can be a dysfunctional place for newly developing relationships. If you want a functional relationship, keep the details of what you're going through, from the first date to becoming an official item off of Facebook and similar social media sites (like Twitter and MySpace).

Key Takeaways:

- 💜 If you're not getting a positive response from your online dating profile, it's most likely because of your photos or the message that you're putting out to the world.

- 💜 Keep your online dating profile succinct and add a little humor when possible.

- 💜 Toss rocks, who only want sex or to take advantage of you, quickly when chatting with men online. Refer to chapter 8 for guidance.

- 💜 When you do start dating a new guy, keep your budding relationship off of Facebook and other social media sites.

CHAPTER 12

Getting Over Being Dumped

*G*etting dumped happens—even when you've done everything right. Some people are just fickle and there's nothing you can do about that except move on. This chapter will help you deal with getting dumped and to understand why it happens.

The 3 Types of Relationships

As I mentioned earlier, one of my favorite transformational speakers is Lisa Nichols, the author of <u>No Matter What</u> and a variety of other works. She said something once that really put things into perspective for me regarding love and relationships.

According to Lisa, there are three different types of relationships:

- 💜 Lifetime
- 💜 Life-Giving
- 💜 For a Time/Purposeful

The lifetime relationship is the one we all search for. The soul mate. That one person who through thick and thin you'll be with forever.

The life-giving relationship is fleeting and short. It's a person who just comes into your life to make you feel alive again, and to let you know that you are still attractive and desirable.

Finally, the "for a time" relationship may last a few months or many years. It is a purposeful relationship, meaning that we either learn something from it (such as our breaking points) or take away something from the experience, such as a child. But unfortunately this type of relationship isn't meant to last forever.

Unfortunately, most people are in "for a time" relationships but don't really know it. They are holding onto the relationship because they are afraid of being alone and don't feel like starting again, but they are only delaying the inevitable. They are not meant to be with that person for a lifetime.

Keep these three different types of relationships in mind as you navigate the dating scene. Understand that you might meet a great guy who gives you everything that you want at the time, but that doesn't necessarily mean that you are soul mates who are meant to be together forever. Don't be afraid to move on when it's time to eventually find that "lifetime" mate—the sooner the better.

Breakups Are Harder on Women... But Only for a Short Time

I believe that getting dumped is hardest on a woman, at least for a period of time. We tend to catch feelings fast and hard, especially after sex. Sex is also very personal to us—we're allowing someone to literally enter our bodies, and in some cases even leave DNA (which is energy) behind. If you know anything about energy, you know that it is a huge risk for a woman to allow someone else's energy into her body. If a man's energy is negative and mean, that can have an affect on the woman he's having sex with. This is another reason why a woman shouldn't have sex with a man unless she knows him very well.

But say that the damage is done and you've been dumped or had to break up with someone who was bad for you... how do you deal with the rejection, shock and hurt feelings that come with it? The answer is different for everyone, but what has helped me was:

1) Deleting the guy's number and blocking him so that I wouldn't be expecting a call
2) Improving my mood by listening to motivational tapes and music,
3) Going out with friends, and most of all
4) Acknowledging my feelings on the matter

I had to cry it out, party it out, scream it out and release that negative energy as soon as possible rather than keep it bottled up inside. Then I would have the clarity to analyze what went wrong. That's important, or else you'll just keep doing the same thing over and over with new guys.

Another solution is to talk to someone new. Have a backup guy to chat with, even if he's just an online friend. You'd be surprised at how quickly you forget about a guy when another interesting, interested guy emails you just to say "hey, how are you doing?"

The plus side of being dumped as a woman is that **women tend to get over a dumping more quickly than men**. And when we do get over a guy, we *really* get over him. We can't even understand why we ever dated him in the first place!

Once you're finally there (it takes time), stand up, move forward, surround yourself with positivity and vow to never allow that type of negativity and pain back into your life ever again.

Tips to Occupy Your Time and Mind with Something Other Than Finding a Man

When you're obsessed with the idea of finding a new man, it tends to bring you more drama and despair than anything. You have to occupy your mind and time with other things in life.

Start a Business or Pursue Your Dream
One way to get your mind off of men is to start a small business on the side. Find something you're talented at and invest some of your time and wages in it. Spend your evenings alone after work refining your business plan rather than feeling sorry for yourself and thinking about the lack of a man in your life. Keep a positive mindset to attract good people in your life (see chapter 9 on the Law of Attraction).

Travel
Another option to consider is traveling outside of the country to experience a wider selection of men. In my opinion, all men have the general hierarchy of values outlined at the beginning of this guide, but it seems that men from *some* other countries tend to be more romantic and traditional (at least in my experience).

Visit a foreign country of your choice, look good, feel good about yourself and get a fresh perspective. If you meet someone you like, test out the newfound knowledge that you've gained from this book—no sex until you have a bond. At the very least, it could give you a self-esteem boost and help you reaffirm your power as a woman.

Experiencing different people, places and things can change your perspective about a lot of things.

Key Takeaways:

- Some relationships are for a time to meet a purpose, some are short and fleeting to give you a boost, and others are for a lifetime. Know the difference.

- Get over a breakup quickly by occupying your mind with something else you love. Remember that women may have a harder time with breakups at first, but only for a little. We tend to be more resilient.

- Consider traveling the world (be safe and smart) if possible to get a fresh new perspective on life and men.

CHAPTER 13

Where I Went Wrong

*B*ack in chapter 2 ("My Story") I gave the stories of three men who basically dumped me. If you'll notice, there is one common thread to my stories—having sex way too soon. Sex changes everything; you can probably relate.

Sex is complicated. For men, it is just an act, a release. Nothing special. For women, it's more. You're giving up something precious and allowing a man to invade your "territory." That's why it's not a wise idea to have sex with a man until you become his friend first and confirm that he's into you as a person, not just an object to be used.

Another mistake I made was being too "eager and willing" with them. I was afraid of being judged as an angry or bitter women, so I played the role of a more quiet and submissive woman instead. That just gave each of them permission to walk all over me.

So as promised, I will go over these three relationships in detail (again, see chapter 2) and tell you exactly where I went wrong.

The Young Sex-Obsessed Guy

If you remember, the young guy I dated dumped me shortly after having sex with me.

The first mistake I made in this situation was dating a guy who was way too young and immature for me. We were in two different places mentally and he wasn't a good catch. He still lived with his parents and had a very immature mindset.

The second mistake was letting *him* decide when we would have sex. That was MY decision to make, not his. That was a clear indication of my eagerness to be with him. I should have said "no" and told him why ("I don't feel comfortable having sex with someone who I'm not committed to"). I should have taken control over that decision.

After sex happened, and he realized that he was holding all the cards, he opted to fold. He bowed out and left me hanging.

The Baby Daddy

The baby daddy is the guy who dumped me coldly after two sexual encounters. He claimed to want to go back to handle his problems with his baby's mama.

First off, I believe the truth is that this guy wasn't really over his baby's mother when he started dating me in the first place. Anyone who has been dating someone on and off for over a decade has developed some strong feelings for that person. He was instantly upset when he found out that she was dating someone new.

Secondly, I should have run when he told me that he had three very young kids out of wedlock while still living with his parents at 30 years old. This is a sign that he's very irresponsible, sexually, financially and in the family planning choices that he makes. He should have been married to his baby's mother after all that time. He gave me the opportunity, but I wanted to give him the benefit of the doubt. I displayed desperation by immediately accepting these terms instead of telling him that I had to think about it. I just blindly accepted these two major red flags. At that point, I should have recognized that *I* was the one who was in a position of power (not too many women would accept a guy on those terms), but instead I gave him a pass and was eager to make *him* feel comfortable.

Thirdly, I made a mistake when I agreed to meet him at a hotel shortly after our second date. I had sex with him too soon, before I had a chance to get to know him more as a person and learn that he had a very childish and flighty personality.

Finally, I made another mistake when I invited him to my home, my serenity, without taking more time to get to know who he was.

I gave up too much of myself too early and the result was that he could take me or leave me. The cards were all in his hands. And when drama with his baby's mother popped up, he immediately decided to leave me. He enjoyed fighting with her more than he enjoyed having peaceful nights with me. That is just how it happens sometimes, and you have to move on.

The Narcissistic City Guy

The narcissistic city guy was the one who lied about his age at first and then eventually ghosted me when I decided not to have unprotected sex with him.

The first mistake again was obviously dating a man who was so much younger than me. He was immature, and that showed by his insistence on not using condoms when having sex with women. In this day and age, who does that?

The second mistake was being too willing to date on his terms instead of my own. I allowed this young guy to tell me how it was going to be, rather than telling him how I wanted it to be.

Here is a perfect example of this: during our relationship, which initially lasted several months, we talked about traveling together. It never actually happened. Then when we reconnected, not long after the breakup I learned that he had gone on a beautiful vacation with some girl who he had just met. Now what was it about that girl that made him *act* on planning a vacation, but for me it was only a conversation? I believe it was that I was afraid to DEMAND what I wanted and she wasn't.

Another point worth noting: this guy admitted to me one day that he wished I would be more passionate, throw things at him and fight with him,. I was very confused by this revelation. I thought, "don't guys want peace and calm in their life?" Apparently not. The young, silly ones want drama and passion more than peace.

So in summary my mistake here was dating an immature guy and being afraid to express myself more. I needed to put my foot down with him on a number of issues. He lost interest and moved on.

All in all, after some time I had to admit to myself that the problem wasn't just them. The real problem was that I was very irresponsible in many of the decisions that I made and in my choices in men. I also wasn't strong enough in my convictions and in telling them what I WANTED.

Today I'm at that point where I ask myself "what did I ever see in those guys in the first place?" But I'm thankful for the lessons nonetheless :-)

CHAPTER 14

Your Turn

I've poured out my heart to you in this book by telling my embarrassing stories of being dumped or used. Now it's your turn to do the same—only just to yourself.

You know the saying, *"those who don't learn from history are doomed to repeat it?"* Well that doesn't just apply to World War I—it also applies to your relationships with other people; especially men.

Another saying: *"Insanity is doing the same thing over and over while expecting a different result."*

This also applies to romantic relationships.

That is why it is so important to look back on your past failed relationships and dating patterns to figure out what you did wrong if you want to avoid repeating bad history. Otherwise you are just setting yourself up to fail the same way time and time again, each time you meet someone new. Something has to change.

So it's time to write your own story. Grab a pad of paper and get to work.

Think back to your last three cases of being hurt by a guy, whether it was a relationship that went wrong after a short time, friends with benefits, getting "pumped and dumped" or unrequited feelings (a guy you really liked who just wasn't that into you).

*Answer the following questions **honestly**:*

1) Which of the items on the hierarchy of men's desires/needs did you meet for this particular guy (if any)?

   - A Looker
   - A Lover
   - A Supporter Who Believes in Him
   - A Friend and Confidant

2) What were his qualities? And which items on the hierarchy of women's needs did he meet for you (if any)?

   - A Protector
   - A Provider
   - A Friend and Confidant
   - A Looker/Lover

3) If you had sex, how long did you wait to have sex with him? Did he make some type of verbal commitment with you before you had sex?

4) When you had sex with him, would you say that you had a bond with him? Could you talk about various subjects on the phone (not just texts) comfortably? Did you know any intimate details about his life and family, beyond the obvious?

5) Who wanted who more? Did he think of you as the prize or did you think of *him* as the prize to be won over?

6) Did you speak your mind and set clear boundaries with him?

7) Did you offer to take on wifely duties for him (such as cooking for him or cleaning up his place)? If so, how long after meeting him? Was he doing anything husbandly toward you?

Now take the answers to these questions to analyze exactly what you did wrong in each situation. Marinate on them for a while. Is there a pattern that you see with each guy you have been with?

Are you being intimate too soon?
Are you too eager to please?
Are you not setting boundaries?
Are you afraid to express yourself?

Are you chasing men?
Are you cooking and cleaning up for him even though he hasn't even made a commitment to you?

The answers to your dating problems are in these questions.

CHAPTER 15

Get Excited

*Q*ren't you excited by the information you just read in this book? You should be! Now you can dry your eyes, get back out there and date with a much clearer mind.

If you're not having luck with dating men and the same scenarios seem to play out time and time again, there's probably something that *you're* doing wrong. Remember, insanity is doing the same thing over and over while expecting a different result! Here is a summary of your dating action plan:

1) Don't have sex with a man without getting to know him thoroughly and having a bond with him. Keep saying NO. He needs to get to know who you are as a person (and vice versa) before getting in your pants. Experience things together. You might learn that you don't even really want him at all.

2) Speak up for yourself! Don't be afraid to voice your opinions and demands to men. You deserve to be happy too.

3) Seek to understand men *and* yourself as a woman more.

4) Look at dating as picking through a pile of rocks to find a jewel. Toss the rocks over your shoulder and out of your life as quickly as you identify them. Avoid the smooth pebbles too.

5) Occupy your time and mind with other things while you're dating. Don't let men overtake your thoughts.

6) Listen to motivational tapes and books about living a better life. This is a great way to occupy your mind too.

7) Work on developing true self-love. How can you expect a man to love you if you don't even love yourself?

8) Use the law of attraction in your life—think and talk about what you want, rather than what you don't want.

Most of all, now that you have this new knowledge, USE IT. Date to have fun. Change up your approach. Maybe instead of being extra polite and chatty with a guy, be a little more brief and honest when you reply to his questions. Tell him immediately when he does or says something that you don't like instead of just nodding your head and acting like it doesn't bother you. When he asks if you are dating other people, instead of saying "well, not really" boldly tell him, "yes, I've met a couple of really great guys!" Instead of being an easy target with a red X on your chest, be a challenge. Be consistent and strong in your convictions.

You may be surprised at the results.

Keep Love in Your Heart

Remind yourself daily to keep love in your heart. No matter how many douche-y selfish guys you have the misfortune of meeting, keep focusing on that one great guy for you. If that's what you really want, keep imaging him in your mind. He's out there and you're attracting him to you every day.

I changed my negative viewpoint about men into thoughts of how many great guys there are out there. The results? My options have increased significantly. I talk to plenty of decent guys. And *I* decide if they stick around or go, which is very powerful.

Fools Rush In

I have a theory that the Internet age has turned us into very impatient people. We rush into everything—dating, sex and relationships. We want to date, have sex, and become a guy's girlfriend in the span of three months. Unfortunately it doesn't always work out that way!

The fact is that the dating to relationship process may take longer than that. The process of bonding with a guy and securing his full attention and affection (and vice versa) takes time.

So again, try to understand that dating should be more of a marathon than a race to the finish line. Finding one man made just for you takes time. Though we live in an instant world, that whole bit doesn't apply if your goal is to build a **healthy long-term romantic relationship** with someone.

Action Plan

After reading this guide, which is jam packed with all sorts of revelations for you to consider in your relations with men, you may feel a bit overwhelmed. You may be wondering where to start.

Here is a simple action plan if you want a real, healthy relationship with a man (the time line is completely up to you).

1. Ask yourself this simple question honestly: **Am I really ready for and open to having a serious relationship with a man at this time in my life?** You

need to ponder if you REALLY want a relationship and for what reasons.

- If yes, proceed to step 2
- If no, take your time, spend some more time with yourself, explore, enjoy your freedom and have some fun in life!

2. **Identify your weaknesses and address each one openly.** You can do this with a trusted friend, a therapist or just yourself in quiet moments. You must rid yourself of negative thoughts and beliefs about your worth as a woman before you can be open to letting an awesome man into your life. You need to exude unbreakable confidence.

3. **Envision the man that you want in your life.** Put him together piece by piece, from his looks, to the way he laughs, to his sense of humor, his kindness, his dedication, his ability to provide and even the way he kisses you in the morning before going to work. Picture it all in your mind. See it. Keep those images there day after day and don't let them go until he materializes in your life. Picture him every morning. Make a place for him in the bed next to you. It may help to create a vision board so that you can remember all of the attributes you want in this man. Be sure that you're asking for the right things, not just superficial things for the wrong reasons.

4. Live your life. Meet new guys, maintaining that picture of the ideal man for you in your mind. Say NO to sex until you have developed a bond, be confident and demand exactly what you want in your dating relationships.

5. Accept your ideal mate into your life.

Also, start to ask yourself these questions each time you are faced with a decision about a man (or anything in life really)

- 💜 How is this benefitting me?
- 💜 Is this going to hurt or help me?
- 💜 Will I feel good about myself?
- 💜 Am I dating this guy for <u>my</u> sake or for someone else's sake (such as a parent or peer pressure)?
- 💜 Am I happy?

Love can and will happen for you. Don't allow yourself to be used for sex or accept friends with benefits arrangements anymore, you can do better. You *deserve* better. You matter. Your needs are important.

Wishing you plenty of love, happy dating and an awesome life!

*If you enjoyed this book or have used it to make a positive change in your life, I'd love to hear your story. Please send your review or experience to **lynngeee9@gmail.com** . It may be published on my website or blog. Thank you!*

Love Lynn

• •

Made in the USA
Middletown, DE
16 March 2020

86500956R00086